businesspartners

successful
communication

For further success in all aspects of business, be sure to read these other businesspartners books:

Successful Interviews
Successful Coaching & Mentoring
Successful Project Management
Successful Time Management
Success in Dealing with Difficult People
Successful Decision-Making
Successful Negotiating

businesspartners

successful
communication

Ken Lawson, M.A., Ed.M.

NEW
HOLLAND

This edition first published in 2009 by New Holland Publishers (UK) Ltd
London • Cape Town • Sydney • Auckland
www.newhollandpublishers.com

Garfield House, 86–88 Edgware Road, London W2 2EA, United Kingdom
80 McKenzie Street, Cape Town 8001, South Africa
Unit 1, 66 Gibbes Street, Chatswood, NSW 2067, Australia
218 Lake Road, Northcote, Auckland, New Zealand

10 8 6 4 2 1 3 5 7 9

© 2005 Axis Publishing Limited
8c Accommodation Road
London NW11 8ED
www.axispublishing.co.uk

A catalogue record for this book is available from the British Library

NOTE: The opinions and advice expressed in this book are intended as a guide only.
The publisher and author accept no responsibility for any loss sustained as a result of
using this book.

ISBN: 978-1-84773-399-3

Printed and bound in Thailand

contents

Introduction

Chances are you know about the party game 'Chinese Whispers'. It begins with one person whispering a thought or observation to another person, who then whispers it to another. The sharing is repeated from person to person until everyone at the party has heard the secret thought. The fun happens when the last person to hear the thought recites aloud the words he or she has heard: almost without exception, the original words have changed, and the meaning of the message has become distorted to a more or less significant degree – often with hilarious results.

Partygoers like to play that game because it demonstrates how easy it is for miscommunication to happen – and for people to be misunderstood. People convey messages differently, and hear them differently. In the workplace, the consequences of miscommunication and misunderstanding can be devastating.

Successful Communication explains how to avoid misunderstandings and build business relationships that are based on an exchange of clear ideas and messages. Through easy-to-read text and a concise, breezy format, you'll understand how effective communication works and learn what you can do to master it in the workplace.

In Chapter 1, you'll learn how communication promotes understanding among people, and how it advances the exchange of ideas. You'll see how effective communication can explain and clarify thoughts, provide direction and extend requests for action. Then, in Chapter 2, you'll read about the many forms of communication that take place in the office, and how to use them to maximum effect in meetings and in negotiation.

Chapter 3 explains verbal communication, and why voice-to-voice exchange is so powerful. You'll also learn why non-verbal communication – gestures, body language and other visual information – shapes our impressions and conveys so much of what we take in as information. Chapter 4 covers written communication, including memos, reports and e-mails, and how to leverage it to your best advantage in the workplace.

Successful Communication offers a wealth of guidelines for mastering communication techniques that work. In Chapter 5, you'll find dozens of tips on effective speaking, including uses of volume and pitch of voice, speed of delivery, vocabulary and emotions. You'll also learn a wealth of effective listening skills, and how they advance the communication process and promote shared understanding between speaker and listener.

You'll learn how to communicate effectively when giving feedback – a critical activity for managers in the workplace. Providing feedback to direct reports (those you line manage) and their experience in hearing it need not be the dreaded event it so often seems; in fact, success in offering and receiving feedback hinges on clear, precise communication.

Finally, Chapter 6 covers effective questioning techniques. You'll learn how to frame questions to elicit information and insight, and use language to maximum benefit in a variety of business situations and contexts.

In the workplace, communication is the foundation for productive relationships among peers, colleagues and reports. As a member of your company or work community, you have an opportunity to develop those relationships to their fullest. *Successful Communication* provides the ideas, strategies and guidelines to help you make the most of that opportunity.

Ken Lawson, M.A., Ed.M.
Career management counsellor and author
Instructor, School of Continuing and Professional Studies
New York University

1

why do we need
to communicate?

Getting the message across

The purpose of communication is to promote understanding; it may or may not have the intention of getting a message across to the intended recipient.

In a face-to-face communication it may not be too hard to promote understanding as you can usually tell by the reaction of the recipient whether the message has been received in the way that you intended.

In a group, though, this perception may be more difficult to ascertain and therefore more care is needed.

The first thing to ensure is that your message is constructed in such a way that the meaning is clear and that it is delivered with clarity. The second is that the receiver has correctly heard and understood.

The message that you do not want to convey is: 'I know you believe you understand what you think I said, but I am not sure that you realize what you heard is not what I meant'. Try reading the sentence again if it did not seem to make much sense at first. Who is chiefly to blame for the misunderstanding?

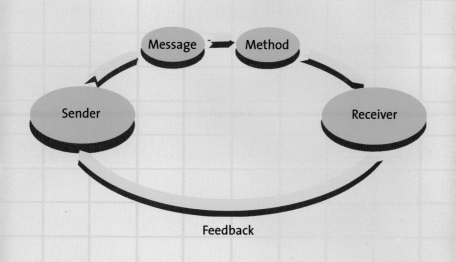

Getting the message across effectively and having it understood is a prerequisite to progression. There is no point in moving forwards if the basic message is lost, or there are barriers in the process. This diagram demonstrates the process.

Benefits of communication

1 Good communication in business is vital to ensure that everyone knows how the company is performing. Company news-sheets can achieve this.

2 Managers should hold regular briefings on the progress of projects, focusing on timing and achievements and to communicate programme changes.

3 Employees have a vested interest in the overall company business but often see only a small part. Managers, especially senior ones, should provide regular briefings.

4 Regular updates from the boardroom help to dispel rumours that persist in workplaces due to misheard conversations.

5 The company's success depends upon an efficient workforce, and efficiency can be improved by good communication.

6   Managers are often quick to point out failings in staff and to criticize the lack of action or bad practice. It is important to praise staff when things have gone well and targets have been achieved. This can be done in department briefings or individual conversations.

7   Good news should be communicated as soon as possible. New orders, increased turnover and good sales results are 'feel-good factors' that will improve morale.

8   Encouraging ownership by the employees will help to improve efficiency and, in turn, output.

9   A good workforce is a major resource, and good communication will make it even better.

10   Bad news is easier to relay when there is a good culture of communication in place.

The feedback loop

Barriers can be encountered at each stage of the process, for example:

1 The sender must establish, or have already established, the credentials that make him or her the ideal sender of the message. If the audience does not acknowledge that the sender is the right person to send the message, the message will not be believed or even understood. For example, news of poor sales should be conveyed by the sales director or even managing director, to demonstrate how seriously management is taking this news.

The sender must also know whether the audience is one person or a group of people.

2 The message must be believable. People will only understand the message if they think it is credible.

The message must be understandable. This often depends on the method by which the message is sent. Possible methods are:
- Verbal, in person or by phone
- Written, such as by letter or e-mail

A message can convey meaning both by what is stated and by what is omitted.

3 The method by which the sender relays the message must be suitable for both the message and the audience, and suit both the message and the person receiving it. Some methods of communication are entirely inappropriate for certain subjects and results.

4 The hearer also has to be considered. The sender should have some understanding of the hearer(s) and of the effect that the message will have upon them. If the method of delivery is not a face-to-face conversation, when will they receive the message?

5 Feedback is important. The sender should elicit feedback from the hearer(s). This will tell the sender that the message has been received and understood. It will also let the sender know how the message was received, and the likely outcome of your action. (Feedback is covered in detail on pp. 182–193.)

6 To be misunderstood in business can lead to costly and time-consuming mistakes. Instructions that are wrong or that are not properly understood can result in abortive effort and that will impinge on the 'bottom line'. Feedback is the way to eliminate misunderstanding.

7 If time is of the essence, pass the instructions verbally but always send written confirmation of the information and ask for a written reply. The writing can take the form of e-mail. This shows a record of the passing of the communication for future reference.

Communicating to converse

Conversing with colleagues is part of normal social interaction. We tend to gravitate to those people who are good at 'small talk'.

Most animal groupings tend to have bonding rituals, and humankind is no exception. Instead of social grooming, we usually bond through conversation. When we are with family and friends, much of the time is spent talking to each other on all sorts of topics. As we spend nearly a third of our lives at work, why should this be different? The cheery 'good morning' called out to colleagues when we first enter the workplace, the conversation around the coffee machine recalling the previous evening's television offering and the comments on the current world situation are all part of the social intercourse that we enjoy with our fellow workers. Rather than distract from the purpose of the workplace, such exchanges help to bond employees together and, as long as they are properly controlled, improve rather than hinder efficiency.

BENEFITS OF WORKPLACE CONVERSATION:

- An occasional break from the routine refreshes the senses and improves concentration.

- Relaxing some of the muscles used in performing the routine task combats strain.

- Talking to a colleague breaks the monotony of a routine task and improves output.

- It improves colleagues' knowledge about each other, and fosters an understanding of their interests outside the workplace.

- A better understanding can lead to an empathy that will improve employee relations.

- A relaxed, refreshed and interested staff works efficiently and improves profitability.

RISKS OF WORKPLACE CONVERSATION:

- It can get out of hand and become prolonged. Abuses must be curtailed.

- It can be a distraction for people who are still working and need to concentrate fully on their task.

- It should not be allowed to become intrusive into people's private affairs.

Communicating to exchange ideas

An exchange of ideas could result from an informal conversation or be part of a structured meeting convened especially for this purpose. Ideas are the seeds that make the business grow, and although they can often seem unrelated to the subject under discussion, they can sometimes be the catalysts for future events or decisions.

Ideas can be exchanged in an informal manner by asking a member of staff for suggestions to solve a problem concerned with their part of the business or, if they seem to have an aptitude for this type of work, for any problem.

During progress reviews or assessment interviews, questions can be asked to exchange information and ideas that can be discussed further and then enlarged upon, in the meeting or at a later date.

Good managers will always be ready to receive information that will improve performance and discuss these with staff at a convenient time.

One of the rules for communicating new ideas is that they should not be dismissed out of hand. Even if they appear unworkable or have been dismissed already, they should be received, and the employee should be thanked.

In a group discussion on ideas, the recommended procedure is to hold a 'brainstorm' session along the following lines:

■ The leader or convenor should state the purpose of the meeting and the subject on which ideas are sought.

■ The members of the meeting should be allowed to offer suggestions that are related to the topic even though the link may be very tenuous.

■ A note-taker should be appointed to capture the suggestions, usually on a flipchart or whiteboard.

■ The ideas should neither be discussed at that time nor qualified, other than to clarify a point of understanding.

■ When the ideas cease to be offered, the duplicates can be eradicated, similar ideas grouped and all remaining items prioritized and discussed in a more structured way.

why do we need to communicate?
Making ourselves understood

Any of the barriers to communication at various stages can prevent the message from being understood. Consider the following:

1 Are you, as the sender, completely clear in your own mind what the message is and how it should be communicated? If you do not fully understand what you are trying to pass on, then there is likely to be confusion. Therefore, you must ensure that you are completely aware of the message and the purpose.

2 If the message is being delivered face-to-face, you need to be certain that your non-verbal or body language is not giving confusing signals. This can be a major problem for the hearer in trying to understand the message. So rehearse the message. Is it logical? Are all parts relevant to the matter?

3 If the message is of a technical nature, have you used jargon, acronyms or abbreviations that are not widely known and understood? This is even more of a barrier if the hearer is not fully conversant with the language used.

4 Is the chosen method of delivery suitable for the type of message being sent? If you are transmitting a complicated procedure or sets of figures that need to be processed before a reply can be given, then a verbal message might not be the best method.

Written down, the message can be read and reread and that way the receiver gets a greater understanding of the problem. (Items of a confidential nature, of course, should be communicated in a protected manner so that there is no chance of the contents becoming public knowledge.)

5 Try to appreciate how the hearers will feel when they receive the communication. What will be the effect of both good and bad news? Will they be expecting something different? Their expectations can help or hinder understanding.

why do we need to communicate?

Explaining

Has a stranger ever stopped you in the street and asked you for directions? Have you ever been tempted to say no or pretend you were new to the area because the task seemed so daunting?

When you had gathered your thoughts and had the directions clear in your own mind, how well do you think you communicated them to the questioner? All those 'Take the first left and then the second right, straight across at the lights' instructions could be most confusing.

Would it have been easier if you had used landmarks – the name of a prominent shop, for example, or a statue – to direct the stranger? This gives him or her a picture to hold onto.

Could you have quickly sketched out directions? This is an example of where the written word is more advantageous than the spoken word. Trying to explain how you want something done or set out can be a problem if you do not use the most appropriate method of communication, in this case a visual image or a sketch.

An exercise to use to highlight the difficulty of explaining something is to have one person with their back to the audience, and without using hands or any other method than speech, to transmit the diagram opposite to the audience.

Without some form of measurement, how do you determine a reference point? The technique is to ask the audience to start by drawing a grid of approximate dimensions. You can then reference the positions of the different outlines and shapes to the grid intersections.

This again shows where barriers can exist in communication. The different results of the exercise show how people receive the message in various ways. This exercise will help to reinforce the notion that not everyone hears the same words in the same way.

Directing

Managers, in particular, communicate to direct the workload of others.

It is a key part of a manager's role to direct the work of others, but many managers find directing staff difficult. This is especially the case if:

■ the task to be carried out is unusual
■ the task adds to their workload
■ the task may mean that they need to work overtime in order to complete it within the required timeframe.

The way the request is made to them will have a bearing on the way they receive it and their willingness to handle the task.

Here we should distinguish between non-assertive, aggressive and assertive behaviour. We will almost certainly have met with examples of all three in our dealings with other people and colleagues.

1   The non-assertive request is usually delivered with either an apology: 'I wouldn't normally ask you to do this, but...' or with too many false compliments: 'I know how good a job you will make of this, so...'.

2   The aggressive request is usually made very bluntly and without explanation: 'I need this back on my desk at 4 o'clock.' Both styles are almost guaranteed to receive a 'no' response.

3   The assertive request is made positively, concisely, but without being abrupt. The reason for the request is outlined, how it has arisen, why it needs to be done and the effect if it is not done. The person to whom the request is directed still has the option of saying 'no', but they now can see why they are being asked.

You may think that assertion sounds like aggression, but there are many differences. In assertive behaviour and communication, you are using your rights and allowing for the rights of your hearers.

Checklist: making requests

Nobody knows it all, especially in a business context. Staff at all levels have to request information from colleagues, superiors, customers, suppliers and others in order to achieve company objectives. Bear these points in mind when making requests.

1 Remember that the way you frame your requests will have a direct bearing on the information you receive. ☐

2 Say 'please' and 'thank you' in your dealings with others. ☐

3 Make clear and understandable requests, and state clearly the reason you are making the request. ☐

4 Make sure that you consider the effect on the respondent of the request. Is the respondent likely to be able to supply an answer? Would he or she know who to refer you to if he or she did not know the answer? ☐

5 Never make a person lose face by your request. ☐

6 State a reasonable timescale for the response to the request and try to communicate the degree of urgency. ☐

7 Say what the format should be for the response. Does it have to fit in with a certain style or layout? ☐

8 Make sure the respondent has all the information he or she needs. Do not withhold vital information. ☐

9 Be available for the person responding to a question so that he or she can clarify or seek further information. ☐

10 Acknowledge receipt of the information and thank him or her for the effort made. If it has meant working outside normal hours, try to arrange some tangible reward. ☐

CHECKLIST

2

communicating in
the workplace

In the department

Communication at work actually starts before you get there. If you live alone, you might not speak until you leave home or the telephone rings, or you give your opinion to the person speaking on the radio who has said something with which you do not agree. If you live with others, you are likely to speak, and will certainly communicate non-verbally. Has a family member ever commented, 'Who got out of the wrong side of the bed this morning?'

From the time we open our eyes in the morning, we can be communicating messages either by verbal or non-verbal means.

Depending on our mood, we either beam at people on the train or bus or bury our head in the newspaper. (This is a useful piece of body language that says 'I do not want to be disturbed'.)

By the time we reach our place of work, external factors mean that we are either full of goodwill towards our colleagues (the sun's shining, the train was on time) or ready to vent our feelings on the first person that we see (we could not find a parking spot, the traffic was heavy, there was a long line at the coffee shop).

1
The way we feel will partly dictate the way in which we communicate and will determine if our communicating is effective. Those with whom we come into contact every day, colleagues, customers, suppliers and others, expect us to function with a high degree of commitment. Our rationale for communicating with the people mentioned is an amalgamation of instructing, informing and influencing.

2
We need to pass instructions to the members of our department so that they can do their tasks in the most efficient manner. We will discuss in future chapters how this can be done. When the pressure is on, passing information correctly, the first time, is of paramount importance. Employees are much happier working when they know and understand what they are doing, and that results from good communication.

3 We need to inform other sections of the progress we are making, for example, whether there are problems that will slow down the throughput of work and what steps we are taking to overcome these difficulties. This information is normally given by sending out a report or by convening a meeting. Customers also expect to be kept informed of the progress of their order, and whether delivery times will be met.

4 The way we speak to our customers and the credibility of the message will influence their willingness to place further business. Your communication with them, by whatever means, could be the determining factor in their decision. This makes effective communication vital.

5 In order to meet the targets you have set, or that have been set for your department, it will be necessary for you to use some influence. (We will consider negotiating skills in more detail in due course.) The amount of influence you have over others will depend on your level of seniority. If you are a junior or even middle manager, your powers of persuasion will be called into play. This could be described as effective communication at its very best.

6 Persuading others to do what you want calls for the use of tact and diplomacy. It requires the correct use of words and will take a good deal of non-verbal skill to achieve the desired result. Any conflicting messages between what you say and what you show in expression or behaviour will be noticed by skilled observers and used to their advantage against you.

7 Using your influence or powers of persuasion will apply equally to other departments within your organization and to outside suppliers. If your company operates a form of Total Quality Management, both suppliers and customers are within your own organization.

8 If you are responsible for the management of staff, you will almost certainly have to conduct interviews. Interviews are required for a range of activities: hiring, appraising, promoting, disciplining and dismissing. In all of these situations, it is necessary to give and receive information to enable you to make the appropriate decision. You will need to bring into play all the listening and questioning skills we will discuss in Chapter 5, pp. 144–199.

Remember that communication is both verbal and non-verbal: it is essential to be aware of everything that is being transmitted, through both means.

To be an effective manager and run an efficient section or department, you need to be aware of the moods and feelings of those under your control. You should be able to interpret the feelings of those working for you by their words and actions. Remember that sometimes those feelings are shown by what they do not do rather than what is said or done. You can normally pick up an air of unease throughout a whole department, but if there is trouble brewing, you need to be attuned to it as early as possible. The following may be indicators of real or perceived problems:

1 Are some of the staff showing any unusual traits or characteristics? Are their behaviours different from what you would normally expect? Do they slam drawers and doors when they leave? Have they been passed over for promotion or had their suggestions ignored?

2 Has a normally very chatty and extrovert person suddenly become quiet and withdrawn? This may be caused by a problem unconnected with work, but it is having an effect upon the way that he or she works.

3 All of these messages, usually non-verbal, need to be interpreted and dealt with. If they are not, the general morale of the workplace will suffer, and questions may be asked about your ability to manage.

In meetings

Most managers would agree that they seem to spend too much of their working days in meetings. But we know that meetings are a very good medium for effective communication. The efficient meeting will:

1 Have all of the right people in attendance

2 Have an agenda that allows full discussion of all of the topics under review

3 Be focused on the matters requiring attention

4 Have set objectives for the resolution of issues

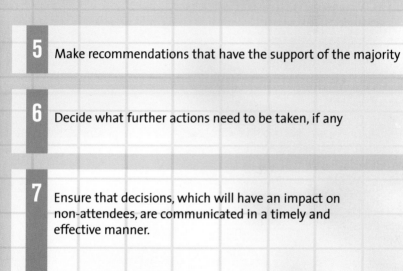

5 Make recommendations that have the support of the majority

6 Decide what further actions need to be taken, if any

7 Ensure that decisions, which will have an impact on non-attendees, are communicated in a timely and effective manner.

That seems like the ideal situation, but unfortunately not all meetings are conducted with this level of control or with this expected outcome. What actually happens will depend largely on the conduct of the delegates who attend the meeting.

The purpose of a meeting is to enable the delegates to express their thoughts and ideas on the topics on the agenda, to try to arrive at a consensus view on those topics and to agree to any actions that need to be taken. These actions may be needed to give the delegates more information or to put the findings into operation.

Before we look at the behaviour of the delegates at meetings, we should establish some practical requirements:

1 Ensure that the venue for the meeting is suitable. The room should be large enough for all the delegates to sit comfortably, normally around a table.

2 Ensure that the room is well lit and ventilated.

3 Provide facilities for delegates to take notes.

4 Provide flipcharts or whiteboards for brainstorming sessions.

5 If the meeting is expected to last for some time, there need to be facilities for comfort breaks.

6 Try to avoid interruptions and excessive extraneous noise.

If you are calling the meeting, prepare an agenda well in advance so that those attending can make adequate preparation.

1 Ensure you have prepared well and that you are sufficiently briefed on each agenda item.

2 Make brief notes on each topic; never rely on memory for facts and figures.

If you are being called to attend a meeting, check when you receive the agenda whether any of the items may require more discussion or are likely to lead to discussion of further issues. Find out from the chairperson if that is a possibility so that you take all potentially relevant information with you.

1 If there have been other meetings on the same subjects, read the minutes of the previous meetings to remind yourself of earlier discussions and check to ensure you completed all of the actions placed against your name.

2 Arrive at the meeting in good time. During the minutes leading up to the meeting, you can either assess the mood of the other delegates by their non-verbal actions, or you can have preparatory talks with some of them to hear their views on certain topics.

3 If you have a choice, place yourself in such a position that you can maintain eye contact with as many other delegates as possible, certainly with the chairperson.

4 Just before the meeting starts, mentally prepare yourself by dismissing as many other workplace issues as you can to allow yourself to concentrate on the meeting.

Much of the success or failure of the meeting will depend on the behaviour of the attendees. Every delegate has a part to play in the smooth conduct of the meeting.

1 Always be conscious of what other delegates are doing. Look around at the members present and consider the way each person speaks, acts and looks.

2 The meeting may not be running smoothly if the following behaviours are in evidence: a person starting to redden at the face and neck because he or she has not been able to make a contribution; someone drums his or her fingers on the table as a reaction to the person speaking; several people speak at once or shout to be heard.

3 Wait until you have made eye contact with the chairperson and have been invited to speak, then make your contribution in a normal speaking voice. Keep your input brief and to the point.

4 It is one of the chairperson's responsibilities to keep an eye on non-contributors and ask for their opinions to draw them into the meeting. If the chair does not do this, you might have to ask for their thoughts on the matter being discussed in such a way that the chairperson does not feel that you are trying to usurp that position.

5 Always allow someone to have a fair hearing even if you do not agree with the view being expressed.

6 Never make fun of someone's contribution in a harmful way.

7 Always try to make what you say add value to the discussion.

8 Never be afraid to change your mind and admit you were wrong, if the facts and the arguments persuade you that it is right to do so.

9 If you do find yourself holding a minority view and cannot in good conscience change your mind, do not be obstructive but allow the majority view to prevail. Time will tell whether you were right to maintain your opinion.

If you convene a meeting and find yourself in the chair, the conduct of the meeting will depend on you and the effectiveness of the communication among delegates will be your responsibility.

1 Think how meetings you have previously attended have been run and what changes you would have made.

2 Try to keep the meeting in order and be aware of the time.

3 Allow everyone the opportunity to speak but not at the same time.

4 Be aware of more reserved individuals and try to bring such persons into the meeting.

5 Make good use of summaries and place actions where necessary.

6 Record the decisions reached and arrange for follow-on meetings if these are needed.

7 Stick to the agenda, allowing sufficient time for the most important items and keep digressions to a minimum.

8 Try to ensure that the delegates leave the meeting feeling that it has been time well spent and that things have been achieved.

communicating in the workplace

In the negotiation process

The art of negotiation is a big subject, and here we concentrate on making our communication within negotiations effective. Current thinking is that negotiations should produce a win/win result with all of the parties being satisfied with the outcome. Try to review negotiations in which you have previously been involved:

1 How much do you give or is taken from you without you realizing that it has happened?

2 When you look back over the process that produced the poor result, can you pinpoint when it went wrong?

3 What did you say that gave away a critical advantage to your opposite number?

4 Perhaps you were suddenly surprised that you had reached your objective(s) in such a short time. What did you say or do that was so decisive?

If you find you increasingly spend time negotiating within the company, or externally with customers or suppliers, now is the time to learn the skills. There are many good training seminars on the skill and some excellent self-help books, but you can make yourself more proficient by rereading the sections on non-verbal behaviours (see pp. 76–83).

Much as we like to think that our use of words is so persuasive that we can achieve anything, it is often what we do not say that has the biggest effect.

Remember that sometimes our non-verbal language contradicts the spoken message. This may be picked up by others and used to their advantage.

This is even more likely when you are confronted with a trained negotiator. They will be watching and listening very carefully to see if there are signs of such conflict and they will seize upon this.

Of course negotiation is not conducted in silence, just through looking at each other's body language. Much of the time is devoted to good discussion, making valid points and, where necessary, giving ground in the interest of progress.

Careful preparation and groundwork is the basis for a successful outcome.

1 Keep the end result in view while at the same time keeping all your available options in mind.

2 If it is a team effort, ensure that all members 'sing from the same songsheet'. If someone steps out of line, the other party will immediately use that advantage to divide the team.

NON-VERBAL BEHAVIOURS TO ADOPT IN NEGOTIATION

1 Always sound and look confident. The two must go together. If the other negotiator senses that you do not fully believe in what you are saying, the argument will be defeated. We give ourselves away in these circumstances by avoiding eye contact. Our speech can become hesitant and we start to perspire. If the room is warm, remove your jacket; do not put yourself in the position that you may perspire naturally.

2 Keep the tone of your voice constant. If we do not fully believe what we say there is a tendency for the pitch of our voice to rise.

3 Keep the speed of delivery constant. If the content of our argument is weak, there is a tendency to speak more quickly.

4 Do not be embarrassed by silence. Keeping quiet deliberately is a good negotiating ploy to see whether the opposing spokesperson will rush in to fill the vacuum and make an unscripted comment. Continue to maintain eye contact. It becomes a battle of wills. Stay relaxed.

5 Do not play with your pen or pencil. This can be taken as a sign of indecision. Touching objects or even self-touching is usually a sign that we are unhappy with the way things are going.

6 Avoid throat clearing and excessive water sipping. These are signs that you are either losing your way or playing for time.

7 Stay calm. Reddening of the face and neck will often suggest that you are losing your temper or are annoyed. This will lead to a loss of continuity in the argument and present an opening for an opponent.

There are occasions where the negotiations are not progressing, neither party is prepared to give ground and the same arguments are being used over again. Now is the time for diversionary tactics.

1 Move on to another subject. Reaching a consensus on some points may mean you can reapproach the stumbling block with fresh confidence of making progress.

2 Always accept the opportunity for a break in the discussions. This will give you a chance to gather your thoughts and marshal the facts again.

3 If you are using a team, be on your guard against being overheard if you discuss progress.

4 During the negotiation, remember the adage: 'It isn't what you say, it's the way that you say it.' This applies to both verbal and non-verbal communication.

Checklist: tips for effective negotiation

1 Draw up your position on all issues, and decide which are the most important in the negotiation. ☐

2 Decide on your ideal outcome of the negotiation. ☐

3 Consider whether you need to change your normal negotiating style. ☐

4 Work out your tactics for dealing with your opponent's negotiating style. ☐

5 Identify where you think your position will overlap with your opponent's. ☐

6 Work out areas where there is likely to be consensus and draw up an agenda accordingly. ☐

7 Identify what your priorities are: your absolute bottom line. ☐

8 Identify where you are prepared to compromise. ☐

9 Have a fallback position ready. ☐

10 Figure out what you are going to say, and rehearse until it sounds totally natural. ☐

CHECKLIST

Checklist: workplace communication

1 Your first communication should be effective: if it is, it will save time. ☐

2 Always communicate problems quickly; delays can cost money. ☐

3 Do not transmit conflicting messages. Ensure that they are understandable and credible. ☐

4 Communication must be a two-way action. You must receive as well as transmit. ☐

5 Always look for and interpret non-verbal messages. ☐

6 Make meetings effective by starting and finishing on time. Prepare, and stay with, the agenda. Publish minutes and actions promptly.

☐

7 Being aware of, and sensitive to, other people's problems does not mean being weak or giving way.

☐

8 Always negotiate firmly but fairly.

☐

9 If a long-term relationship is desirable, try to achieve a win/win outcome to negotiations. But do not give away essential items.

☐

10 Always live to fight another day. If agreement cannot be reached, then reconvene for another time.

☐

CHECKLIST

verbal and non-verbal
communication

Types of communication

We communicate with our whole being: with our gestures, our eyes, our facial expressions and our moods, as well as with our voices. We communicate throughout the whole of our lives, from the cradle to the grave. With almost our first breath, we told the world that we were there with a yell and eventually, we will all breathe our last words.

DEFINITIONS OF COMMUNICATION

A general definition of communication is 'the art of passing information and ideas from one person to another'. This definition, however, misses one vital element in the process. The definition should have said: 'the art of passing information and ideas from one person to another so that they can be received in the manner they were meant'.

Communication is both verbal and non-verbal. A breakdown of the way in which we communicate our meaning shows that, in percentage terms:

1 The actual words used convey 7 per cent of meaning.

2 The tone of the words conveys 38 per cent of the meaning.

3 The body language conveys 55 per cent of the meaning.

The most important part of effective communication, therefore, is not what you say but the way in which you say it and the attitude you adopt when you deliver it. In other words, we must try to understand the coded signals that make up 93 per cent of the actual message.

We all know how confusing it is if someone says one thing but seems to mean something else. You are absolutely sure that you fully understood what was said but at some later point the individual tells you that you have not understood a word. This is frustrating for both parties.

1 Where did the confusion arise?

2 What part of the overall message did you not understand?

3 Whose fault was it?

Verbal communication

The easiest part to get right might appear to be the spoken word; it is the smallest part of the message, and most people would say they were good with words (although many people are not). However, for the moment, we will ignore tone and body language and concentrate on the verbal content.

As someone in a management role, you have to get other people to do the tasks of your department or section. If you do not communicate your requirements clearly, without ambiguity, and understandably, these tasks will either not be accomplished or could contain errors and omissions.

It was once said:

Three-quarters of all verbal communication is lost, or ignored or misunderstood IMMEDIATELY.

The remainder is forgotten within a few weeks.

Oral or verbal communication, therefore, requires the words to be heard and understood. It is a two-way process and involves a 'transmitter and receiver'. This is very much like a radio broadcast, except that when the sound waves leave the radio transmitter, there is no way of knowing if they have been picked up by the receiver.

The radio receiver in your possession has to be activated first. So it is with effective communication; the person with whom you are trying to communicate has to be ready to listen and prepared to receive your message.

The sender is the one who has to take responsibility to see that all is prepared. Too often we assume that what we have said is what has been received, but this is not always the case, and when things are not done, or done incorrectly, we often blame the hearer of the message. Look at the following example:

WHEN I SPEAK, YOU	AS A RESULT YOU REPLY
■ Hear what I think I said	■ What you think you said
■ Hear what I said	■ What you did say
■ Hear what you think I said	■ What I think you said

These are the possible outcomes if we do not ensure that the hearer has properly understood the message.

The two-way process

We have already established that communication is a two-way thing, from sender to receiver, and a confirmation back from receiver to sender. But if that is all that happens, things can go wrong. The communication ladder should have a few extra steps if it is to be effective. When the receiver hears the message, it has to be interpreted by the brain:

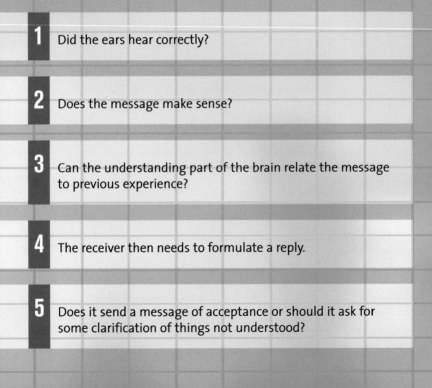

1 Did the ears hear correctly?

2 Does the message make sense?

3 Can the understanding part of the brain relate the message to previous experience?

4 The receiver then needs to formulate a reply.

5 Does it send a message of acceptance or should it ask for some clarification of things not understood?

The sender now hears what the receiver has replied and needs to interpret the response to see whether it correlates with what was originally sent.

1 Does the reply make sense to the sender?

2 If it does not, where does the fault lie, with sender or receiver?

Although this concept has taken some time to explain in detail, the actual process is over in a couple of seconds.

EXAMPLE

Employee: Your message on my voicemail said that you wanted a sales report similar to the last one.

Manager: Yes, please.

Employee: But your comments on the last one suggested a different format, which should I do?

Manager: Oh, sorry. I would like you to break the sales figures by area, and by quarters, with a percentage increase or decrease compared to last year. Is that OK?

Employee: Yes thanks, now it is perfectly clear.

verbal and non-verbal communication

Results of poor verbal skills

The phrase 'art of communication' is often used and, like any art or skill, communication has to be practised and practised until it becomes second nature.

1 So much time can be lost in the office or the workplace because of poor communication.

2 So many tasks can go wrong and so much wasted effort can result because the message did not get through.

3 You must check, preferably more than once, that the message has been received and understood and interpreted in the way that it was meant.

4 Although it can be very frustrating to have to repeat or rephrase the message for the benefit of the hearer, try not to show any impatience.

5 If your subordinates believe that you can humiliate them with sarcastic remarks because they do not understand first time, they will attempt to do what they think the task is and not what you intended.

6 This will be frustrating for you and will most probably mean that they will lose motivation.

EXAMPLE

Manager: (to all staff) These reports that you've submitted are useless; they do not give the information I need.
Employee: But your e-mail wasn't clear on what it was you wanted.
Manager: Well then, why didn't you come and ask me?

Employee: Because you make sarcastic remarks if we ask for clarification individually. If you were to come into the office and explain it to everyone involved in person, we could then ask if we did not understand you. It would save time.

Style and tone

One of the principal reasons we use verbal communication in business is to persuade: we persuade our subordinates to perform the tasks that have to be done and persuade our customers to purchase our products or services. But the power of persuasion does not rely on just the spoken word.

We all know that if you put the emphasis on a different word in the same sentence you get a totally different result. There is a title of a song that says, 'What is this thing called love?' Try putting the emphasis on each word in turn, and you get six different meanings.

The tone of voice used is very important to convey the correct meaning of the message. If you want a live example, just listen to a sports commentary on the radio – you can judge the excitement of the event by the commentator's voice; the greater the excitement, the higher the pitch and vice versa.

1 A dictatorial or hectoring tone will suggest that you are trying to browbeat or bully the listener into doing what you want. As a manager, you would not raise your voice or shout at someone if you were trying to express sympathy for something that had happened either at work or in the person's private life. Your voice would tend to be at a lower pitch with a regular rhythm and a fairly slow rate of delivery.

2 Communicating the importance of either the whole message or just part of it is best done by the choice of words rather than the volume. People who are angry tend to raise their volume level and pitch. Their words are clipped and the delivery is fast.

3 If you need to ask for a job to be done and you know that it will be unpopular, do not adopt a whining or wheedling tone. Remember what was said about assertive behaviour and, in a natural tone, give the reasons why the job has to be done by the person chosen within a certain time frame.

EXAMPLE

Manager: (shouts) Where were you yesterday? There was an urgent job to be done.

Employee: I'm sorry but you said I could go to see my brother who is seriously ill in hospital.

Manager: Did I? Sorry, I forgot, oh yes I remember now. How is he? Keep me informed, please.

Employee: Yes I will, thanks. What is the job to be done?

Manager: Are you sure you are ok to do it, can you concentrate?

Employee: Yes, I'll be fine.

verbal and non-verbal communication

Body language

We refer to those silent signals we give as body language, but it may be better to term them non-verbal expressions because they can be more than deliberate or involuntary movements of the body.

1 More than half of our everyday communication is done by body language. We can use it to reinforce the message we are trying to give.

2 Using verbal and non-verbal language together and correctly is a very powerful way of communicating. If, however, the two signals are at variance with each other, the message is confusing and garbled. The receiver is at a loss to identify the true meaning.

3 What should be believed – the message that is spoken or the message that is signalled? It is important that we should listen for the words and look for the visual signals.

4 When we communicate face-to-face, we must use our ears and our eyes to receive and understand the complete message.

There are several ways in which the non-verbal behaviour reacts with the spoken word.

1 COMPLEMENTING A verbal message can be delivered in a flat monotone, devoid of emotion and feeling, but it can be enlivened by facial expressions. It is almost impossible to hide emotion in the voice if you smile, either with your mouth or your eyes. It is also possible to complement what is said by using a slight forward leaning of the body or a hand gesture. These can be used to show both pleasure and displeasure either with the listener or with a third party. Be aware that sometimes our non-verbal signals can contradict instead of complement the verbal message.

2 REINFORCING By repeating the words with an appropriate gesture, we give the hearer a double message. For example, when we give directions, not only do we give a string of instructions but we can also point or describe by hand movements the correct course.

3 EMPHASIZING We can accentuate what is being said by nodding or shaking our heads or using hand gestures.

4 SUBSTITUTING It is possible to signal to someone and have them understand without a word being said. There is the 'thumbs up' or 'thumbs down' sign for yes or no. The arms can be used to welcome or repel. We raise our eyebrows to show surprise or knit them to register our displeasure.

We are often at pains to suppress our feelings and not let them show. There is a perception that a display of emotion is a sign of weakness – we may fear that we will be 'punished' in some way if we let our feelings show, that we might be considered 'too soft' for the role of manager or supervisor, or that we may be unable to make tough decisions when necessary.

In general, we have much more control over our verbal communication than we have over our non-verbal communication.

1 Many non-verbal signals are involuntary – for example, we blush when we are embarrassed; we perspire freely when we are afraid or when we are not being truthful.

2 While we may be able to control our words, we are less capable of controlling our non-verbal actions. Having said that, our feelings and emotions will often seem to be powerful signals, sometimes more powerful than the spoken word; we must guard against reading too much into these alone. It is essential that we look at both types of signal to interpret the message correctly.

3 In interpreting non-verbal signals, it is important to consider the time, the place and the person. A smile given to a member of your family or to a colleague in the workplace, for example, will usually signal a happy disposition, that you are pleased with someone or something. A smile given to a member of the opposite sex when sitting in a railway compartment may be totally misinterpreted.

4 It is said that a picture is worth a thousand words, and body language can be used like a picture. Effective use of body language can save lots of verbal dialogue and will give a much better impression than the spoken word. A warm verbal greeting is much more convincing when accompanied by a pleasant outward appearance. Praise means a lot more when given with warmth, and good body language gives this impression of warmth. Eye contact reveals much more than the words coming from your lips. Take a moment to look in a mirror and see how your face will change when you attempt different moods. These expressions will occur when you speak to people and are often responsible for the first impression you make on people. Try to practise the different styles of body language discussed throughout this book, and learn when to use them to best effect.

The term 'body language' involves the whole body. The face reflects and projects our thoughts, but the whole body send signals to those we are speaking with or to.

As a simple example, many of us have been to a lecture, or sat in a meeting, when the lecturer or chairperson constantly jangled pocket change. This is a typical gesture for someone who is unused to speaking in public, or uncomfortable being the centre of attention. It is not only distracting to an audience, it also gives the wrong message. The message that comes across can be that the speaker is uninterested, bored or even dishonest. However good the verbal communication, the body language in this case lets it down. At the end of the meeting, the overriding impression left on the audience has nothing to do with the words.

GESTURES

Gestures can be divided into intentional movements, where we are deliberately making a signal to convey a specific meaning, sometimes coded, and involuntary movements, which we use to reinforce our words.

Television studios use various gestures to convey, wordlessly, instructions from the director to the performer. Hands roll round each other in a forward movement to signify that the performer should keep going. The open hand drawn across the throat is an instruction to whoever is speaking that they should 'cut' the oration as soon as possible.

There can be cultural problems with gestures as signals can mean different things in different countries. In some parts of the world, for example, showing the soles of the feet can be insulting. Before business trips to countries with which we are not familiar, it is advisable to try to obtain information on any possible pitfalls so that a single careless gesture does not ruin carefully planned negotiations for future business.

Hands and feet

When we are communicating, our hands tend to do all sorts of things; most of these movements are involuntary.

1 We sometimes put our fingertips together, almost as if in prayer, to show that we are concentrating.

2 We clench our fists, not in preparation to hit someone but often to prevent someone else from intervening in a conversation or discussion.

3 Self-touching that often takes the form of supporting the jaw or the head when it is tilted slightly to one side is another involuntary gesture. This will often signify that we are concentrating on what is being said.

4 Object touching, by contrast, is a gesture that often denotes worry or fear: we touch things that are close to us or that are in our pockets or a handbag. Often they are personal objects that give us support because we feel comfortable with them.

CONSIDER, TOO, THE HANDSHAKE.

1 A handshake can be cold and formal or warm and responsive.

2 The formal handshake tends to be loose and limp, whereas the warm handshake is very firm and is often held for a longer time.

3 Shaking hands can be a cultural custom, too. In some cultures, handshaking is almost a ritual that is done at the point of meeting and departing.

It is not just by using our hands that we send messages: tapping a foot can be a sign of impatience as can shuffling our feet.

A wrinkled nose can suggest that not all is well and show our displeasure or even that the environment is not to our liking.

Posture

The way we stand and the way we sit can convey feelings in a similar manner to other non-verbal signals. The way we sit when in conversation can reflect to the speaker how attentively we are listening (see pp. 154–165), whether we are absorbing the information being transmitted or hearing but not understanding.

1 Slouching back in a chair can signify that we are not really interested in what is being said and that we would rather spend our time doing something else.

2 Sitting with our arms and legs crossed suggests that we really do not want to get too involved in what is being said and that we are holding ourselves aloof. It can also be interpreted as a sign of rejection.

3 Sudden changes in posture signal a change in our major concern.

4 Sitting upright following a slouched position signals that we are now interested and intend to get involved in the subject on hand. The reverse sequence would suggest that we have now lost interest or find the subject tedious.

5 When we stand, the way we stand will give signals; we tend to stand in a more upright position when in conversation with someone we perceive to be of a higher status than us but strike a more relaxed pose if it is a subordinate.

Appearance

It is said that we communicate vital information in the way we present ourselves to other people and in the way we dress and adorn ourselves. There are still remote tribes in some parts of the world that paint designs on their bodies in lurid colours. This is intended to instil fear into opposing groups and to try to avoid physical confrontation. In all societies, there are people who attempt to do the same in their style of dress.

Consider your response if called to attend an interview, either for a new job or for promotion within your organization. You take some trouble with your appearance, if only to comb your hair if called upon at very short notice. We attempt to look smart to give the impression that we are smart – in our minds as well as in our appearance. We all like to give a good impression of ourselves, and our physical appearance is the first clue we give to someone when we meet them.

1 What sort of impression do you get when you meet someone whose appearance is scruffy and unkempt? You may feel that they do not care about you.

2   If potential suppliers came to see you to discuss some important business deal looking as if they had come straight from house painting, would you consider them to be serious about the meeting?

3   'Power dressing' and designer labels might suggest that the wearer is more affluent and therefore has a higher social status.

For this reason, many companies, especially Japanese companies, have adopted a 'uniform' for their employees to wear. It suggests that everyone is of equal importance to the company. They do not want there to be any false layers of superiority.

4   Of course, your first impressions may be entirely wrong; we must guard against relying on those initial ideas. However, having made them, we are likely to be coloured by them until other factors cause us to change our mind.

Placement of furniture

This may seem a strange item in a section on non-verbal communication, but the way we place furniture in a room can have a major influence on effective communication.

1 Consider, for example, the United Nations Security Council meeting room. The table is horseshoe-shaped and the senior delegates sit at the table with microphones and headsets. The advisers sit on an outer ring of chairs at the shoulders of the delegates. They cannot participate in any conversations or discussions except at the invitation of the senior members.

2 Furniture can be a barrier in other ways. The placement of a desk or table between you and other parties will signify that the occasion is formal or that they could be worried by the reaction of the listener and so need some form of 'protection'. To relieve the situation chairs should be placed so that there are no barriers between all participants.

3 In a conference room, a long table with parallel sides will mean that all those sitting on one side will be on the same plane and unable to communicate with those further away from them. Even if they can manage to speak to each other, there will be little eye contact and so more than half of the communication will be lost. It could result in passing notes to each other, communicating by writing, which is something we will deal with in due course.

4 When you are making a presentation, regardless of the size of your audience, be aware of the furniture. This includes chairs, tables and any visual aids that you might use. If at all possible, check the venue ahead of time. Consider the following factors:

- Are the chairs comfortable, and for how long?
- Do your listeners need tables for work sessions?
- Can everyone see your overhead projector screen?
- Is the projector blocking the view of some of the audience?

You may not have control over the animate objects but you can control and use the inanimate objects to your advantage.

Putting it all together

To take a common example from business life, we will consider the job interview. You have advertised and shortlisted the respondents and now you have to interview them face-to-face. It can be a daunting experience for both parties and advance planning is necessary for both.

1 Aim to be relaxed and try to put the interviewee at ease. So much more can be extracted when the person feels comfortable.

2 Have the chairs arranged on the same side of the desk; do not put a barrier between you from the outset.

3 Make sure that there are facilities for interviewees to leave coats and bags outside the interview room so that there is no flustered removing of coats in the interview room.

4 Stand up to greet interviewees as they enter the room. Make eye contact and shake hands firmly. Look and sound interested from the moment someone enters the room.

5 You will have read their CVs before they arrive and will have made notes of any questions you want to ask or points that you want them to enlarge upon. Set an agenda for the interview, and let the interviewee know what you intend. For example, 'I would like to ask you about your current position and some of your previous experience. I would then like to hear your views on why you think you are a good fit for this position. Finally, there will be an opportunity for you to ask me any questions.'

6 Ask open questions to give interviewees a chance to express themselves so that you find out whether this person is right for your needs. Open questions, generally, are those that start with How? Where? When? What? and Who?

7 Give the impression that you are interested even if you have decided early on in the interview that the person is not the ideal candidate.

8 Be prepared to clarify any questions the interviewee is unsure about so that you do get relevant answers.

Checklist: communication

1 Speak clearly and concisely to convey your meaning carefully. ☐

2 Make sure that the message is received and understood. ☐

3 Be aware of your feelings when you communicate. ☐

4 Be aware of the effect that you have on the person receiving the message. ☐

5 Look for body language, both in yourself and in the listener. ☐

6 Remember that 'body' means the whole of you and not just your face. ☐

7 Be sensitive in both word and expression. ☐

8 First impressions are often those we remember the longest. ☐

9 Imprecise communication is one of the great time-wasters of the business world. ☐

10 Non-verbal communication accounts for 93 per cent of what we communicate. ☐

CHECKLIST

4

written and electronic
communication

The written word

We use written communications in business for a variety of reasons – most especially when we want to have a more permanent record of what has been said or done.

1 Although contracts can be verbal, it is more sensible if they are written and signed.

2 Reports can be delivered by word of mouth, but they are usually requested in a more formal way. Presenting a written report allows the recipients to study it in greater depth, and it is available for future referral.

3 Minutes of meetings are written and circulated to attendees and other interested parties – sometimes on paper, by e-mail or in some other electronic form.

4 Even with the increase of electronic communication, it is still a recognized practice in many industries to contact customers by letter.

The written word confirms and reinforces conversations held either face-to-face or by telephone. Memories are fallible and, as we know, ambiguities and misunderstandings can arise. In all written communications, we should aim for six things:

1 ACCURACY

Ensure that what you write is correct. This refers to facts, comments, figures, times and schedules. There is no point in communicating inaccurate information. Always check the veracity of the information before you commit it to print.

2 RELEVANCE

A great deal of time can be wasted if we give our correspondents useless information. At best, this leads to further contact to question, clarify and then correct the misinformation. At worst, your customers or suppliers will act on your information to their own detriment.

3   BREVITY

We should aim to be brief but not to the detriment of accuracy. Most managers do not have the time to read through reams of information and want something 'snappy'. When writing a report, always start with a summary of the contents so that busy people can quickly see whether they should continue to read or if the subject matter is something that can be passed to a subordinate.

4 STRUCTURE

Minutes of meetings should be a summary of the main points of the meeting to remind the readers of the matters discussed, the action that needs to be taken and the people responsible for action. They should never be a verbatim report of all of the business discussed.

5 CLARITY

Never lose clarity by being too brief. To be understood, statements need to follow in a logical progression, and each step should be explained, especially if the information or argument is complicated. Keep paragraphs short and focused.

Acronyms and other abbreviations should be shown in full when used for the first time, and thereafter in each section, because not all your readers will read a report from start to finish; instead, they will access those portions they need.

6 AUDIENCE

In a longer document, it can be helpful to include a summary of the main points at the start, in the order in which they are discussed. It is also a good idea to include a glossary of terms at the beginning of the document. This will act as a point of reference for readers when unusual terms are used throughout the submission. Try to avoid jargon unless you know that all the readers are conversant with such terminology. Scientific and technical reports are particularly susceptible to this.

The various forms of written communication need to be looked at in more detail if the communication is to be effective.

written and electronic communication

Letters

Before committing anything to paper, we should plan carefully. Keep in mind the following:

1

WHAT SHOULD THE LETTER DO?
Consider the reason(s) for writing. Do you want to inform, to complain or to congratulate? The purpose of the letter will help to determine the style and tone.

2

WHAT SHOULD THE LETTER CONVEY?
Has the intended recipient already had a letter or other form of communication from you? Is the content something with which they are familiar? What is the mood that you are trying to set? Remember that there will not be any form of eye contact or body language for the reader to assess the way that you are feeling; it all must be conveyed in the writing.

3 WHO IS THE LETTER TO?

If you know the intended reader well, then you will usually adopt a friendly tone, or an informal manner. If the letter is in answer to one received from them, the tone and style of their letter could be reflected in your reply.

4 WHAT IS THE STYLE OF THE LETTER?

The style of letter writing has changed considerably over the last decade. The very formal language of writing is now usually practised only by the legal profession. Try to avoid long-winded or pompous phrases; instead of 'We acknowledge receipt of your communication dated...' write a simple 'Thank you for your letter of....' Wherever possible use short words rather than long ones. It is unusual to use very formal phrasing in communicating verbally, so it is advisable to avoid it in writing.

5 WHAT IS THE FORMAT OF THE LETTER?

The convention for the format of the letter has also changed. Now it is acceptable for every line to start at the left margin of the paper; even the date and the closure are now left aligned. It is a good idea to quote a reference that the recipient will recognize and also to head the letter with a reference to the content. This will help to ensure that, when writing to a company not an individual, the letter will be directed to the appropriate person or department.

EXAMPLE OF OFFER OF EMPLOYMENT LETTER

April 10, 20XX

Dear X,

We are pleased to offer you the position of sales representative at our Cityville branch. A formal contract of employment will be sent to you in the next few days for you to sign and return. In the meantime, we confirm the main terms of your employment.

The position is as sales representative, level 2, at an annual salary of X, paid monthly. The appointment is subject to a three-month probationary period, at the end of which, if successfully completed, the appointment will become permanent.

A bonus on all sales over X per month will be paid at 0.5% of the amount by which actual sales exceed the target. This will be payable after the trial period has been completed.

You will be required to work a basic 37.5 hour week with 20 days per year paid holiday.

We look forward to welcoming you into our team on Monday May 1, 20XX.

Yours sincerely,

Internal memos

Company 'memos' are normally installed on computers in a format that suits the business.

1 As the name implies, internal memos are intended for use within the company.

2 As such, memos are informal communications between staff.

3 Because memos are composed on and sent by a computer, the contents can become common knowledge unless some security protection is employed.

4 Given that different people within the company can read them, it is best to avoid including any comments that could be misinterpreted by other members of staff.

MEMORANDUM

To: Liz Longfellow
From: Gordon Griffin
Date: April 15, 20XX
Subject: Monthly sales figures

This is to remind you that the next sales review meeting will be held in my office on Friday May 2, 20XX at 10.00 am. We need to review the sales for your 3 areas for the month of March and to look at the trends for the past 2 years.

Would you please project sales for the next 3 months by both area and product line. I am sure that the management team will ask for these and we want to be prepared.

If you have any problem obtaining up-to-date figures, let me know at least a week in advance and I will contact the accounts department for them.

Thanks,
Gordon

written and electronic communication

Writing reports

One of the most frequently performed tasks in the world of business is report writing. Reports represent an important part of effective communication within an organization. They allow information to be transferred among different departments and to individuals within those departments. There are various reasons for writing reports, among them:

1 To record the progress and results on a task or project

2 To provide financial information

3 To set out proposals for discussion

4   To collect thoughts and ideas from interested parties and present them in a manner that all can readily access

5   To present statistical information in a variety of formats, from tables and simple pie charts through to complex, comparative charts and diagrams.

The nature of the presentation, formal or informal, will depend on the format of the report and also on the status of the recipients. For reports that will be sent outside of the organization a formal layout is usually required. Internal reports can be informal.

Both types must strive for accuracy, brevity and clarity (see pp. 100–103). To ensure that the report will be read and understood, we need to set some guidelines. These should include:

OBJECTIVE SETTING
Before you commit anything to paper, decide what the objective is.

1   If there is more than one objective, how do they relate to one another?

2   Should they be dealt with separately, or can they be combined without any of them being lost or ignored?

3   If you have been asked by someone else to write the report they should have given you objectives to follow.

From all of the information available to you, what items are essential to the report? Too much information and the length of the finished report will deter readers from actually finishing, thereby missing some vital information.

1 Your objectives should provide the frame upon which the details can be added.

2 Try to consider what the reader wants to know. How much information do they already possess? Are they all at the same level of understanding?

3 What do you need to achieve when the report has been read?

4 Poor objectives will produce a rambling report, and your objectives will not be met.

CONTENT
Given that an unduly long report will deter the reader, the detail should be considered carefully. The report must follow a logical sequence and the steps marshalled correctly so that the arguments or statements flow.

1 Do not give a conclusion if the intermediate steps are missing; the reader will wonder how you arrived at the conclusion and may dismiss the report as flawed.

2 Graphic information (charts, tables of costs, diagrams) is an important part of the report and will reinforce the written word.

3 Decide whether graphic information should be included in the body of the report or placed in an appendix, with the necessary references stated in the report. If the finished report is quite long, it may be best to use an appendix so that the readers can get the gist of the information to enable them to form an opinion.

Photographs may form part of an appendix, if they add to the understanding of the report (make sure that they are referenced or marked to show the relevant detail).

 Always acknowledge any references to other contributions.

LAYOUT

The report should not be an ego trip for the writer but a source of information for the reader. Just as we appreciate some form of signposting when we are travelling, so does the reader of a report: readers need to know where the report will lead and what they will encounter on the way.

1   If the report is to be externally distributed, then the front cover should be attractive.

2   It must clearly state the title and the author's name.

3   A short title is best to establish the content; use a subheading to add to the meaning.

4   A contents page that lists the sections will assist readers in finding the relevant information. It could be that some readers will be interested in certain parts, and a reference to where that information is to be found is vital.

5 If the report is more than just a few pages long, number each page and add these to the contents page. To help the reader further, a summary of the report should follow. It should condense the whole report and as such will often be the first item the reader looks at.

6 The main body of the report should be broken down into paragraphs, sections and subsections, each one referenced either in an alpha or a decimal system.

7 Each section should follow logically and contain sufficient detail for the reader to comprehend.

Many people have acquired the art of speed reading. This requires text that flows in a sequence, enabling the reader's eyes to skim down the centre of the page while absorbing the words on either side. Whether or not your readers expect to be able to speed read the report, it is annoying to have to reread a passage, perhaps more than once, to fully grasp the meaning. Much of this can be avoided if the style is crisp and the punctuation logical.

Conclusions must be placed at the end of the report and should be based on the content.

1 Do not draw conclusions from outside sources or material not contained within the document. The report's content should point logically to the conclusion that has been reached. Show whether alternatives were considered and list the factors that led to them being rejected.

2 Recommendations can be made from these conclusions. These could be solutions or plans for further work, or a note that more research needs to be undertaken before a 'real' conclusion can be reached. Recommendations can include a time frame, if appropriate.

Well-written and well-presented reports have a standard format, and always include similar subheadings. The example on the opposite page has a well-used structure for a report.

CONTENTS	Page

1. Terms of reference 1
(This gives brief reasons why you have undertaken the report and the objectives for it.)

2. Summary 3
(This will be written after the main body of the report and will be a synopsis of the content.)

3. Introduction 4
(This gives the background, history, any exceptions or assumptions.)

4. Main body of the report (using subheadings) 6
(This should state the current situation and analyze the steps taken and the possible solutions together with costs and benefits, using numbered paragraphs such as 4.1, 4.1.1, 4.1.2, 4.2, and so on. At this stage do not make recommendations.)

5. Conclusions 10
(These are based on the findings of the main report.)

6. Recommendations 11
(These are made on the findings and conclusions in the report.)

7. Appendices 12
(Any information, such as references or extracts, that is not of immediate use to the reader should be given at the end of the report.)

The decimal system used above is widely used because it makes for easy referencing. A glossary of terms used in a technical report should be included. Never assume that the reader will understand jargon and acronyms. Always check to see if your company has a preferred format for reports.

Minutes of meetings

Whether a meeting is informal or formal it is a good idea to keep a record of what happened. This serves as a good point of reference for subsequent meetings as well as a means of settling any disputes that might arise over the content of the meeting. Whoever is appointed to record the meeting by taking the minutes should capture the most important matters.

1 Minutes of meetings should include: where and when the meeting took place, who attended and who did not attend, the topics discussed, the actions arising from the discussion and who is to take the action, the decisions that were reached and the plans for the future, such as further meetings or reports to be submitted.

2 It is not necessary to record the meeting verbatim, but it is important to give sufficient information to remind those present of the discussions and business that took place.

3 A draft set of minutes should be given to the chairperson for approval before they are printed and distributed to members. This should take place some time before the next meeting is scheduled.

EXAMPLE OF MEETING MINUTES

Minutes of the 18th Sales Management Team held on Thursday April 13, 20XX at 10:30 a.m.

PRESENT
James Wood, Sales Manager; Jo Smith, Northern Area; Frank Wright, Southern Area; Jane Phillips, Eastern Area

ABSENT
Don Read, Western Area

ACTION
The minutes of the 17th meeting were approved and signed.

MATTERS ARISING
James reported that the changes to the sales area boundaries had been approved by the board.

SALES AREA REPORTS
Reports were presented by the three representatives present, and these were discussed. It was decided to ask Don to submit a written report to the other members by April 24. DR

SALES TARGETS
James stated that the CEO had agreed to meet with the team to set out the targets for the next sales year. It was agreed that too great an increase could be a disincentive to sales staff. James agreed to send a brief to the CEO apprising him of these thoughts. JW

SALES CONFERENCE
The date for the conference has been set for October 18 and 19, and the venue will be the Midland Hotel, Derby. Area managers should notify all of their staff. VS, FW, JP, DR

There was no other business, and the meeting closed at 12:30 pm.

Graphical presentation

Charts and graphs are an important part of communication because they present figures in a form that allows easy comparison and relationships.

1 Most people are familiar with pie charts and with bar and line graphs. These are frequently used to illustrate figures. Most standard computer programs will turn columns of figures into a chosen chart format and allow these to be imported into the report at the appropriate place. If they can be printed in colour to differentiate between the areas, they become even more effective.

AREA	QTR1	QTR2	QTR3	QTR4
North	10,000	15,000	12,000	10,000
East	20,000	15,000	15,000	20,000
South	8,000	9,000	10,000	11,000
West	1,000	1,000	1,000	5,000
TOTAL	39,000	40,000	38,000	46,000

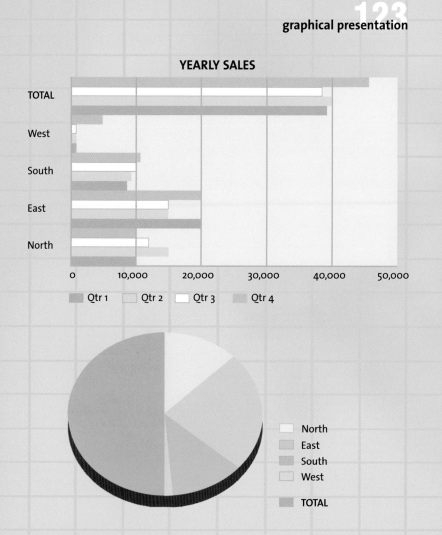

YEARLY SALES

2 Other equally valuable communication tools are flow diagrams. These show the logical sequence of events that must be undertaken in order to complete a given task or project. Some are fairly simple or straightforward, but others are very detailed and complex and must be generated and controlled using a computer program. Among the foremost of these are the PERT chart and the GANTT chart.

FLOW CHART

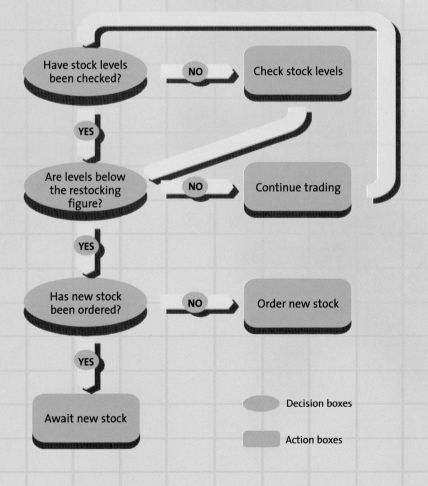

3 The PERT chart takes its name from Program Evaluation and Review Technique. This will analyze the critical path through any task and calculate the maximum time estimated to completion. It will also show which tasks can be done in parallel to avoid delays. It is a very specialized procedure, and there are training manuals and computer programs written especially to facilitate writing. The review is done on a regular basis and shows where program slippage has or will occur. The PERT chart is a very effective 'stand-alone' planning tool.

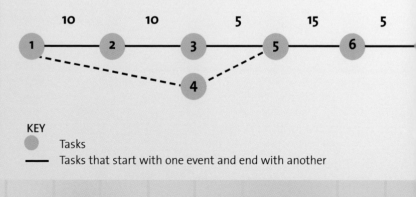

KEY

● Tasks

— Tasks that start with one event and end with another

The PERT chart below shows the sequence of events involved in producing a company report.

1 Gather relevant information
2 Write and edit copy
3 Review by board
4 Source photographs
5 Design and page layout
6 1st proofs produced

7 Correct 1st proofs
8 Proofread and check 2nd proofs
9 Review by board
10 Final corrections
11 Make pdfs for printer
12 Print and bind

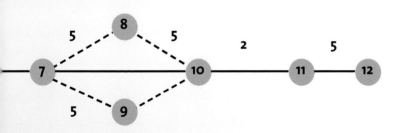

- - - Events that depend on completion of other tasks

5 No. of days

4   The GANTT chart, named after Henry L. Gantt, an American
    management consultant, is a similar but simplified way of
    detailing the steps required to complete a task, showing their
    relationship to one another and an estimate of the time each
    step should take. The aggregate of times for every step will
    give the overall timescale. With this system, it is necessary to
    review progress as a regular feature and correct any estimates
    that have proved to be false. The cumulative time can then be
    adjusted. The GANTT chart can be included in a report or used
    as an independent model.

GANTT CHART

PROJECT: LAUNCHING A CALL CENTRE IN INDIA										
ACTIVITY/TASK	**TIME/WEEKS**									
	1	2	3	4	5	6	7	8	9	10
Put recruitment ad in newspaper/website	▢									
Set up interview		▢								
Appoint home-based India representative			▢							
Research equipment suppliers and costs					▢					
Find India-based coordinator					▢▢					
Buy/rent office space in Jaipur					▢▢					
Buy/lease and install equipment									▢	

▢ Duration of task

Advertising

If your business is in either the manufacturing or service sectors, it is important that you are as widely known as possible.

1 Advertising can take various forms: newspaper ads, brochures, flyers, billboard posters and mass mailings. Each of these is a form of written communication and, if they are to be effective, they must make a quick impression.

2 All written communication should be **interesting**. After all, it needs to hold the reader's attention throughout the document. It should also be **informative** – the reader should have a greater knowledge of the subject after reading the document than before – and it should **influence** by making the reader respond. Through these three **i**'s the writing should be effective.

3 As with other forms of writing, the objective(s) must always be kept in mind. The main objective is to grab the attention of the target readers and to make them want more information.

We have all seen ads or posters that have made an impression upon us either through the content, the humour or the image. It might sometimes be wise to use the expertise of an advertising agency. This will be more expensive, but the results should be worth it.

4 More people are now shopping via the Internet and browsing through web pages to find the products or services they require. The main thing about web advertising is the need to be found. It is easy for 'household names' to be found. If you are not in this category, you can pay to get yourself noticed. If you are unwilling to do this, opt for gimmicks: moving images, bright colours and so on. It is worth paying a professional to make sure your site links work first time. Visual clarity is important: some colour combinations and typefaces work better than others for text. Consider the age of your intended audience and size type to fit. You can also offer video downloads.

written and electronic communication

Electronic communication

We might think that electronic communication only covers e-mail and text messaging by mobile phone, but of course the telephone is also a form of electronic communication.

The telephone is still very often the first point of contact between companies and between companies and individuals.

CALL CENTRES

There has been a huge growth in telephone call centres where businesses have outsourced their customer service departments. This is often done to reduce overheads by using cheaper labour.

The call centre service has been automated to such a point that it can often be frustrating. Always remember that customers have a choice, and if they are frustrated too often they could take their business elsewhere. Large conglomerates may not be concerned about the loss of one customer, but if it becomes a flood of dissatisfied customers, the loss can cause the business to collapse.

DO'S AND DON'TS OF WORKING IN A CALL CENTRE

- Do answer the call promptly.
- Do be pleasant when responding to queries.
- Do be sensitive to the caller's circumstances.
- Do allow for nervous or confused callers.
- Do ensure that the choices offered cover all types of query.
- Do put yourself in the position of a caller to test the system.
- Do not lose your temper.
- Do not lose your patience.
- Do not give misleading messages.
- Do not put callers on hold unless you know you can get back to them promptly.

TEXT MESSAGES

Text messaging is perhaps not a good medium for business communication. (There is a story of one firm that informed its employees by text that the company had gone into liquidation and they no longer had jobs.) It may be a useful way to send informal messages between colleagues, but it can be discounted as a serious means of business communication.

written and electronic communication

Telephone

One of the drawbacks to telephonic communication is that even though it involves words and tone, the major part of how we communicate non-verbally is missing. Even so, it is more effective than written communication. The tone of the conversation is important: does it sound friendly and interesting? Does it sound as if the caller is happy to talk to you?

1   What sort of impression do you make on the telephone? If you are the first point of contact, you are the 'ambassador' for the company, and any future business might depend on the way you sound to the caller.

2   Always talk clearly on the telephone because the system has the ability to distort messages that are not clearly enunciated. If a word or words are difficult to understand, ask for them to be repeated.

3 If the person you are calling is unavailable, leave a message asking him or her to return the call and give a convenient time. If you will be out of the office or workplace for lengthy periods, let them know when you will be available because it is very time-consuming to keep returning a call only to find the other person is not there.

4 Take care when leaving messages on answering machines. If you have been connected to the wrong number (and it does sometimes happen), that person can phone back to tell you. Your communication will not have been effective if you have left it with the wrong person. Always state the day and time of your call, give a brief idea of what the call is about and repeat your telephone number just in case the message is interrupted and not fully received.

There can be no set script for a telephone conversation as each is unique with regard to the content and the result. If the call is a form of complaint, it is wise to remember that although the customer may not always be right, he or she is always the customer and you may want to keep their business.

Consider the following:

Good morning/afternoon, could I speak to Mr/Ms A.B.

My name is Sam Smith of XYZ Electricals. Your message said that you have a complaint about one of our products.

(A.B.)...

S.S. I'm sorry that fault has occurred, it is most unusual but I'm sure it can be repaired. Is it still under guarantee?

(A.B.)...

S.S. I realize that you are disappointed, and I apologize. Can you bring the appliance to the shop so that we can test it?

(A.B.)...

S.S. It would be better if you could bring it to us because we have all the necessary equipment here.

(A.B.)...

S.S. Whenever it suits you. We are open until 6pm this evening and until 8pm tomorrow.

(A.B.)...

S.S. Certainly, if it cannot be repaired, we will replace it.
(A.B.)...
S.S. I will see you then and we will work out what can be done. Once again, can I say how sorry I am, and thank you for bringing this matter to our attention.

You could try to solve the problem on the telephone if you think that it might be a simple problem but referring to wiring diagrams and complicated mechanisms can be daunting to the average customer. Never enter into the 'blame game' on the telephone.

Internet and e-mail

THE INTERNET

The Internet has opened up business communication to a degree that could only have been dreamed about a decade ago. It is now possible to download all sorts of information from news about the stock markets to the times of flights to any destination. You can book a hotel room and pay for it and buy aircraft tickets and book the seat that you prefer, all from the computer keyboard. And using the various 'news services', up-to-date information on business trends can mean instant decisions on the best course of action to take, thereby minimizing any detrimental effects on your business.

Of all the progressive steps taken in communication over the last 20 years, the development of the latest electronic methods have revolutionized the way we communicate in business. Universities are now running courses in e-commerce looking at all the techniques that can be deployed, even to the setting up of virtual companies that have no physical existence, no premises and no permanent workforce. They exist purely in the 'ether', and yet they do business and generate vast profits. They communicate with one another and with customers by electronic means in a highly effective way. This would seem to be the commercial future, but just how much further it can go we can only guess.

E-MAILS

You may recall or have been told how difficult it used to be to do business with companies internationally. The time differences between the United States, Asia, Europe and Australia made telephone conversations almost impossible. It would take days to ask and answer questions.

Now, with e-mail, communication around the globe is almost immediate. The transmission of documents can be just as fast, allowing negotiations to be undertaken and concluded in a much reduced time frame.

Using e-mail has also speeded up internal communication and should reduce the amount of paper used on internal memos and information transfer. The 'paperless office', however, still seems to be some way off. One other advantage with e-mails is that, unlike a telephone call, they do not have to be dealt with straightaway: a response can be considered.

E-mails are now widely used to communicate both formally and informally. Although some employees have sent flippant and/or scurrilous messages to their colleagues, abusing the system, the internal e-mail has largely replaced the internal written memo. An e-mail is quick and convenient and has the advantage that it can be hard-copied if required.

There are some formal occasions when an e-mail is not suitable as a business communication, and these include sending items of a personal or confidential nature, contractually binding documents and others requiring a personalized signature.

For e-mails to be effective they need to follow the rules of good letter writing and be well structured, grammatically correct, and devoid of spelling shortcuts such as those used in mobile text messages.

E-mail attachments are a very useful adjunct in that pictures and diagrams can sent to amplify or back up the written word. This can be extremely useful for diagnostic purposes and product recognition.

This procedure will usually involve the use of a digital recording system that can be linked to the computer.

The advantages of using e-mails, where appropriate, follow:

1 Offers speed of transmission

2 Lets receiver read messages at a convenient time

3 Is less expensive than the postal service

4 Is more accurate than a telephone message

5 Allows one message to be sent to as many people as required

6 Enables 'conference communication' in various time zones

7 Keeps the business traveller in touch with home base

written and electronic communication

Checklist: types of communication

The following points should be remembered:

1 The written word is still important and, in some cases, essential. ☐

2 Strive for accuracy and brevity, but tell the reader/listener what he or she needs to know. ☐

3 In all forms of communication, clarity is the principal aim. ☐

4 Always plan what you are going to say and stick to it. ☐

5 Keep to the point and be logical; it aids the reader because he or she avoids rereading the material. ☐

6   'A picture can be worth a thousand words'. ☐

7   Make good use of modern technology, but use it appropriately. ☐

8   When using the telephone, try to imagine the effect you are having on the other person. ☐

9   The telephone can distort your voice; speak clearly and at a reasonable pace. ☐

10   In all forms of communication, you are trying to inform; don't leave your readers/listeners more confused than they were. ☐

CHECKLIST

5

how we communicate

We communicate when we speak

Faced with the question 'When do we communicate?', many people would answer: 'When we are in conversation with someone or when someone writes to us or we write to them'. So it would appear that we communicate with the use of words, either spoken or written. This is usually the case in business life.

But consider the mime artist. Without saying a word, he can make you 'see' the room in which he is supposed to be: point out where the furniture is; show you what the weather is like in his world; indicate whether he is hungry, happy, sad, old or young. He can make you believe he is contained in a glass box when in fact he is uninhibited. Gesture, expression or emotion convey all this information. These are also means of communication, tools you use all the time, sometimes without realizing it and sometimes in direct opposition to what you are saying. It is almost as if you are shaking your head while saying 'yes' and nodding while saying 'no'. If your words and gestures are giving conflicting messages, what is your hearer to make of the communication?

We still need to communicate when experiencing the following emotions:

1 When we are happy or sad.

2 When we are pleased or angry.

3 When we want to be heard, and when we want privacy.

Each of these emotions will affect the way we think – about ourselves and our colleagues – and the way we act and therefore the way we communicate with them.

The spoken word

We discussed in Chapter 1 how a message leaves the sender and travels by a chosen method to the hearer (see diagram on p.13). The most common method is the spoken word. But our words may be coloured by a variety of factors. We should consider some of the ways that change how our words are being produced and how this can affect the way in which our hearer(s) receive them.

VOLUME

1 Talking in too soft a voice will mean that people may not hear the complete message and wonder as to its true meaning – the clarity of what you are saying is lost. If they only hear part of it and are required to communicate the content to other people, what will the result be?

There is a party game in which a sentence in whispered into the ear of the first person, and it is passed from person to person until it returns to the sender. Very often the final message is different from the original. You may have heard the classic example where the original sentence was 'Send reinforcements: we are going to advance' and the final version was 'Send three and fourpence: we are going to a dance'. It can be fun as a party game but very damaging in a business context.

2 If we speak too loudly, it might be interpreted as aggressive and may antagonize the people for whom the message is intended. A raised voice suggests intimidation or bullying.

PITCH

1 Delivering at the correct pitch for your audience is an important part of a lecture or presentation. Too high and it can sound piercing and uninteresting; too low and it can become inaudible.

2 Dropping one's voice at the end of a sentence can make one appear uncertain.

SPEED OF DELIVERY

1 We think faster than we speak, and we speak faster than we can hear and comprehend. Therefore, we must ensure that we have marshalled our thoughts correctly and present these thoughts in word form without a garbled delivery.

2 If we want our listeners to act upon what we tell them, then we need to choose a pace that will allow comprehension or note-taking. A short pause between sentences allows your hearer(s) to see the relationship between your ideas, and this leads to better understanding.

VOCABULARY (CHOICE OF WORDS)

1 Never underestimate the intelligence of your hearer(s) or try to use obscure words or phrases. The *Complete Oxford English Dictionary* contains more than 600,000 words. Our average vocabulary is between 3,000 and 5,000 words. Most people manage to convey meaning using this reduced number.

2 Sometimes it is necessary to use technical words or jargon. If you think that there could be someone who does not fully understand this form of terminology, then do take time to explain.

3 Unless everyone is fully conversant with acronyms or abbreviations, avoid using them. Also remember that some acronyms are known differently in other countries. For example, the initials NATO, standing for North Atlantic Treaty Organization used in English-speaking countries, is OTAN in France, Belgium and Spain.

EMOTIONS

1 The way we feel will affect the way in which we communicate, and this will affect the perception of our audience and the level of understanding given to our message.

2 We cannot always choose the time at which we need to convey our requirements so we must try to control our emotions when speaking.

BACKGROUND KNOWLEDGE

1 It is always dangerous for speakers to assume that hearers will have sufficient knowledge of the subject to enable them to fully comprehend all that is said.

2 Speakers should try to find the extent of their listeners' understanding of the subject.

3 The structure of the presentation or lecture should ensure a logical progression; otherwise, the audience will be distracted by trying to marshal the information into the right order and will most probably miss some of the content.

4 Always plan carefully before delivering the finished article.

We communicate when we listen

So what is the skill in listening? Isn't it something that we have done all of our lives? Surely it is one of those intuitive skills that we acquire? 'If I hadn't listened at school, college, university, work, I would not be in the position I am today.' Just so! But how well have you listened? What have you missed along the way?

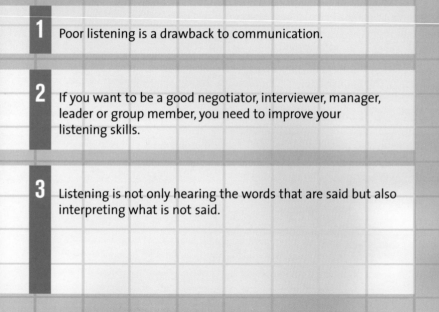

1 Poor listening is a drawback to communication.

2 If you want to be a good negotiator, interviewer, manager, leader or group member, you need to improve your listening skills.

3 Listening is not only hearing the words that are said but also interpreting what is not said.

Is there something missing from what you are being told? Do the expressions and body language of the person speaking seem to be at variance with what they have said? You have most probably been challenged with 'You haven't heard a word I said!' when you have mumbled or grunted in reply to a message. That person is almost certain to be right for you have not concentrated your attention fully on the speaker; you have heard the words but have not understood them.

We know that different people can hear the same message in different ways. This may not always be a problem, but if misunderstanding should happen during a negotiation, we could lose a competitive advantage – with costly results. In an interview, to mishear or not understand a candidate's reply could have serious consequences on the outcome.

Types of listening

How do we improve the quality of our listening? In their book *Social Skills in Interpersonal Communication* (2nd ed.), Hargie, Saunders and Dickson identify four main types of listening:

1 **COMPREHENSION LISTENING** This is the kind of listening we use when we are fact-finding or note-taking.

■ Listening to a lecture, for example, in order to be better informed about a subject that we may want to refer back to at some future date.

2 **EVALUATIVE LISTENING** This is used when we are being persuaded by an argument and we have to judge whether what is being said is something that we are prepared to accept.

■ A party political statement, for instance, or any kind of advertising feature.

■ A proposition where we need to identify the strengths and weaknesses.

3 EMPATHIC LISTENING   This is trying to understand the message from the perspective of the speaker.

■ Understanding the whole message contained in words, feelings and attitudes.

4 APPRECIATIVE LISTENING   This is the type of hearing that gives us pleasure.

■ Hearing the things we want to hear, sometimes to the detriment of the whole message.

Listening prejudices

What influences our ability to listen correctly in any of the four ways listed earlier? Sometimes our prejudices can prevent us from listening and comprehending the message. These can include:

1 AGE
We may think that the speaker is too young to have sufficient knowledge. Or the listener could be too old and not be conversant with the latest thinking on the subject.

2 GENDER
In some cases, people may think that either gender might not be qualified in regard to certain subjects or situations.

3 RACE
Something that may have affected our way of thinking towards people of certain races may cause our attention to wander from the message and its understanding.

4 SOCIO-ECONOMIC STATUS
We may pay more attention to a person perceived to be of
a higher status than one from a lower status.

5 APPEARANCE
We are told 'not to judge a book by its cover' but we can
allow appearance to divert our concentration from the
message. It may be a physical characteristic, the style of
dress or the demeanour of the speaker.

Factors that influence listening

DELIVERY
The speaker's delivery will also affect your ability to listen effectively.

1 The normal rate of speech is between 150 and 200 words per minute (although people can speak more quickly than that).

2 We can manage to listen and comprehend at a rate of 500 to 600 words per minute.

3 Our attention can wander during the gaps, and if it wanders too far, we can miss the next important part of the message.

4 The more interesting or novel the message is, the greater our concentration span will be.

5 Its complexity will also have an effect.

EARLY CONCLUSIONS

We can have a tendency to arrive at a conclusion having heard only a part of the message and start to formulate a reply.

 Even though it is only a thought process, it can close the mind to the remainder of the message, and the true meaning may be lost.

 Effective listening means that we must give the speaker our full attention before we start to think of an answer.

EMOTIONS

If the speaker is having trouble controlling his or her emotions (anger, sorrow, despair) and they are distracting from the message, we may be so involved with these emotions that they become more important to us than the message itself.

 Try to give the speaker time to vent these feelings.

THE FEELINGS OF THE LISTENER

If listeners feel motivated either by the subject or the speaker, then their attention span is often greater and reception more acute.

1 The harder it is to listen, the more difficult it will be to understand the message.

2 If the listeners are not well or are tired or are not seated comfortably, this too will detract from their attention span.

3 The time of day is also a factor in productive listening. Speakers do not like to present in what is called 'the graveyard shift', the period after lunch or dinner.

4 Being able to make sense of the message is also an aid to concentration. If the listeners must 'translate' what they hear, either because the subject is unfamiliar or of a difficult technical nature, comprehension will be affected.

BACKGROUND KNOWLEDGE
Comprehension is lost if there are parts that are not understood.

1 If the subject of the presentation or lecture is not well known, listeners may need to do some background reading in advance to gain an idea of the subject matter and some of the technicalities involved.

EXTRANEOUS NOISE
Concentration and understanding can suffer if the speaker is struggling to be heard over noise from outside the room.

1 Air conditioning units, fans and heating systems can generate a loud hum, and a room next to a busy workplace or a road will also cause problems.

2 It is also important to ensure good ventilation so that listeners do not become sluggish.

Listening skills

ACTIVE LISTENING

Although listening is a sense that most of us are born with, to do it well takes practice, patience and perseverance. Although it is something we have been able to do since childhood, we have all been accused at some time or other of not listening to the speaker. We may have repeated the words that we received, but we have not actively listened to what was said.

1 The active listener can respond to both the verbal and non-verbal communication, to what was implied and inferred.

2 The active listener hears what the speaker says and feels.

Educational theorist Keiran Egan in his 1998 paper 'Concepts of Development in Education' identifies four basic listening skills:

- attending
- listening
- empathy
- probing

And we can add another:
- reflecting

Before we look in more detail at these skills, there is one important consideration and that is to prepare ourselves for listening. There are three ways to do this:

1 Arrange a suitable time. Not only must you find time when there are no other pressures or commitments that will intrude upon the time set aside (which in itself must be adequate for the occasion), but also as a listener you should be at your mental best. Tiredness or fatigue will impede active listening.

2 Arrange a suitable environment. Choose a room that is light and airy. Make sure that you will not be disturbed. Remember to switch off mobile phones.

3 Do some research in advance. Find out some background information about the speaker. What is his or her interest in the subject? What do you know about the subject? Read any notes that may have been issued in advance.

Attending

It is now possible to look in more detail at the basic listening skills. They should apply mainly to face-to-face listening, but some of them could be applied to groups as long as the seating has been carefully planned and arranged beforehand.

1 ATTENDING

Active listeners pay attention to what is being said and convey the correct impression that they are genuinely interested in the speaker and the message. Such attention will develop a rapport that will enable the speaker to be more forthcoming and give a fuller account.

We cannot help but give out clues about how we are feeling with our body movements and posture. This needs to be practised: take the opportunity to sit with a colleague and, choosing any topics, take turns at speaking for a couple of minutes while the other tries first not to listen and then to listen attentively.

After trying both roles, examine the signs that were visible in each case.

SOLER EXERCISE
This exercise will highlight the non-verbal communications that take place.
Trainers and coaches use the mnemonic **SOLER** as an aid to show that the
listener is receptive.

S: FACE THE SPEAKER SQUARELY

1 This position tells speakers that we are paying attention to
them and are with them.

2 Do not sit so rigidly that speakers feel overpowered by
too much attention but do not turn too much to the side so
that it looks as if you are not interested and wishing that you
were elsewhere.

3 Looking out of a window or at a notice board shows that you
are lacking in concentration.

O: ADOPT AN **O**PEN **P**OSTURE

1 Do not sit with arms and legs tightly crossed. This suggests that you want to keep the other person away from you and that you are not interested in what they have to say. Try to have your hands uncrossed and resting on your lap unclenched. If you must cross your legs, do so at the ankles.

L: LEAN

1 Lean slightly towards the speaker with the upper part of your body, but not too far forward as this will appear intimidating.

2 A slight lean tends to show interest and attention.

3 A skilled listener will know when to lean and how far, according to the speaker's attitude and approach.

4 However and whenever you lean forward, do not go so far as to encroach into the speaker's 'personal space'.

5 Do not lean back or slouch, as this will be taken as a sign of boredom with the speaker or the subject, or both.

E: MAINTAIN GOOD **E**YE CONTACT

1 Although it is necessary to maintain good eye contact with the speaker, this does not mean that you should stare fixedly. This will give the impression that you are trying to dominate.

2 What is described as a 'soft look' at the speaker will show that you are listening and are interested. You do not have to look the speaker in the eye all of the time. An occasional glance at his or her hands if the speaker is gesturing or a look at his or her notes if the speaker is sitting opposite you will cement the feeling that you are paying attention.

3 Try not to look away for long periods or peer over the shoulder of the speaker. This is likely to give the impression that you getting bored.

4 Try to keep a pleasant, neutral expression on your face, rather than a fixed grin.

5 To have no eye contact at all suggests that you have no interest and would rather be elsewhere.

6 Do not look at your watch or the clock on the wall. This will suggest that you do not have more time for the speaker.

7 If you find that looking into someone's eyes is embarrassing, try looking at the bridge of their nose. Except from very close up, they will think you are looking at their eyes.

8 It is advisable not to take notes during a face-to-face interview because this takes your eyes away from the speaker.

9 Arrange to have a separate question-and-answer session when the entire message is complete.

R: TRY TO BE RELAXED

1 Do try to adopt a relaxed attitude when listening. If you are fidgeting and seem tense, the speaker will assume that you are not interested and cannot wait to be elsewhere.

2 Avoid appearing too relaxed because this will have a similar effect upon the speaker. By sitting comfortably and looking alert, you will project an air of interest in what is being said.

All of these techniques need to be practised so that they feel quite natural when you are listening. This is more important when there are just two of you.

Empathy and probing

Empathic listening is listening from the perspective of the speaker. To achieve this, the listener must look for all of the signs, verbal and non-verbal, that will give an indication of the state of mind of the speaker. There may be a pause or fading of the voice or a wistful look.

1 This is the point at which the effective communicator will offer a 'door opener' to the speaker. Useful phrases such as 'You seem to be finding this part difficult', or 'Do you want to stop for a moment?' will show that you have identified the mood and are trying to help. Never feel inclined to say 'I know just how you feel' because you do not. If the door opener does not work, just pause and allow the speaker to carry on with the original message.

2 A word of warning: there can sometimes be a fine line between empathy and sympathy. Empathy is feeling into another person, in a neutral, objective manner. It is more typically appropriate to active listening. Sympathy is feeling with another person in a non-objective manner, and is not always appropriate to active listening. Always be aware that, in some cases, you may be given a 'sob story' to encourage you to take a more lenient approach, especially in something like a disciplinary interview.

PROBING

This is both a questioning skill and also one of the skills that the listener needs to ensure that they have all of the required information.

1 It could be that the speaker has assumed that you have a greater knowledge of the subject than is the case, or that he or she has sidetracked from his or her prepared notes and left a gap.

2 The listener needs to do some gentle probing to elicit the vital piece(s) of information. These are usually called clarification probes and take the form of 'What exactly do you mean?' or 'Do I understand that...?'

Checklist: listening

1 To listen properly, you must both interpret and understand. What is really being said. Is it a coded message? ☐

2 Listening is done with ears and eyes. Remember the spoken word accounts for only 7 per cent of the message. ☐

3 We need to listen to both facts and feelings. It could be the speaker's or our feelings that might change the message. ☐

4 Do not be prejudiced by outside factors such as age or appearance. Let the message come through unfiltered by false assumptions. ☐

5 If you are in doubt about what you think you heard, then ask questions. If you do not understand one part, other parts may be lost. ☐

6 Try to be in the mood to listen and be aware of your own feelings.

☐

7 Do not jump to conclusions too early in the message. Wait until you have heard it all and then reach a decision. If in doubt, clarify.

☐

8 Be attentive. Pay attention to all that is being said, both verbally and non-verbally. Try to maintain eye contact.

☐

9 Do not do other things at the same time you are listening, unless it is taking brief notes for future reference.

☐

10 Evaluate what you have heard and seen. Does one contradict the other?

☐

CHECKLIST

Reflecting

Nothing is worse for the speaker than to have someone repeat his or her every word. It either sounds like a bad echo or a clever parrot in the room.

1 Reflecting is a way of paraphrasing what has been said to show the speaker that you have heard and understood the message. The ability to reflect is useful in both presentations and interviews. It should be used sparingly but effectively.

2 Reflecting should encompass both words (content) and feelings (effect), and the listener must be very aware of the effect the message is having on the speaker.

3 This technique shows comprehension and understanding and will prompt further information. Reflecting is intended to demonstrate that the listener grasps the speaker's content and effect, and is now ready to progress to the next level in the conversation.

4 Paraphrasing covers the content part of the message. The listener responds, in a concise manner and using his or her own words, to the essence of the message.

5 Reflecting feelings covers the affect part of the message. We are not very good at conveying our feelings except in a negative way, that is, by leaving them out of the spoken message. The skilled listener looks for these hidden statements and uses them to establish the true facts. This is achieved by reflecting the perceived feelings of the speaker. Using an expression such as 'You appear to be annoyed by that. What is the reason for that?' will hopefully bring out some reasons. An expression such as 'Were you pleased, because…' will contain reflective responses for both content and feeling. If you have misread the unspoken clues, the speaker will rebut your reflection and then you can establish what was the true feeling.

There are various phrases that can be used to clarify or reinforce the understanding of a spoken message. It is also a useful ploy when you need speakers to enlarge upon statements they have made.

Phrases such as 'If I have understood you correctly, then…', or 'Can I just make sure I've understood, you said that…', will either confirm your understanding or will enlarge upon a previous statement.

6 One thing to avoid is to say 'I know exactly how you feel...' because, unfortunately, you do not. This can often be said when a colleague or an employee comes to you with a personal problem. We think we know the answer and fall into the trap. It is acceptable to say 'I can imagine how you are feeling...' and then continue with 'but what effect is it having on you'. They may or may not tell you.

7 Summarizing can be used to break up the message into easily digestible parts. At a convenient break point, for example, when the speaker pauses to take a breath or to look at his or her notes, the listener can summarize what has been said so far. This is also done in the listener's own words and is a useful reinforcement of understanding for both speaker and hearer.

Feedback

Most people think they know all there is to know about themselves. They have a good idea about the way they present themselves to the people whom they meet, both by their words and their actions – in other words, by what they say and do not say. In fact, quite often this is not true, and what they say or the way they behave has a 'grating' effect upon the listener.

1 By giving feedback, we are literally 'feeding back' to someone what you think or how you feel about an aspect of his or her speech or behaviour.

2 Feedback offers the person information about him- or herself that will enable the person, if he or she so chooses, to develop a different way to present him- or herself.

3 The 'Johari Window' was developed by Joseph Luft and Harry Ingham as a model to illustrate the way in which feedback can be given based on four kinds of information about us. An adaptation of their model appears on pp. 184–185.

FEATURES OF THE JOHARI MODEL

1 'OPEN' QUADRANT
This quadrant represents things that you know about yourself, that others also know, such as your name and job title.

2 'BLIND' QUADRANT
In this quadrant are things that other people know about you, but that you might be unaware of. For example, you may rarely make eye contact with people you speak to, but not realize that this is a problem for the people you deal with regularly.

3 'HIDDEN' QUADRANT
In this quadrant are things you know about yourself but have not disclosed to others. For example, you may not have told colleagues you are married or have small children.

4 'UNKNOWN' QUADRANT
These are things that you do not know about yourself, and that others do not know either. You might prove to be an able squash player, but if you have never tried the game, you will not know this.

INFORMATION KNOWN TO SELF AND TO OTHERS

INFORMATION NOT KNOWN TO SELF

INFORMATION NOT KNOWN TO OTHERS

OPEN AREA

HIDDEN AREA   BLIND SPOT

UNKNOWN

INFORMATION NOT KNOWN TO SELF OR OTHERS

- The two blue circles on the left show the information we already know about ourselves.

- The two blue circles at the top show what is known to other people, i.e., what is common knowledge.

- The bottom left blue circle is the information about ourselves that so far we have not shared with others.

- The two blue circles on the right show information we do not know about ourselves.

- The upper right circle depicts information known by others, of which we are unaware.

- The lower right circle shows areas of our lives that are unknown to us and to others and will always remain so, even though this circle will get smaller as we discover more about ourselves and share that information with other people. (The circles have been shown as the same size as each other, but their relative sizes can and do change, as more information becomes known.)

By giving feedback, we are helping to remove some of the blind spot by revealing information we have gathered from what has been said or done.

For feedback to be effective, it has to be accepted by the person receiving it.

1 It needs to be factual, specific and about what has happened.

2 It is split into two parts: the behaviour and the effect, that is, what the person has said or has done, and the effect it has had.

3 The effect is what you say, do or feel in response, or what you know someone else to be saying or doing.

If someone has written a report and he or she is inexperienced, to say 'That was good' will be of no help. Instead you should indicate what was good about it and how it came across to you, saying, for example, 'The introduction made it clear what the report was about and what you expected to be the outcome. It made me want to read it' or 'I found the structure logical and easy to follow.'

If the feedback is related to someone's behaviour, then it is even more important to separate the facts from the opinions. If your feedback to the chairperson of a meeting was that he or she was a good chairperson, this is your opinion, not a statement of fact. Consider instead:

1 What did he or she do that was good for the meeting?

2 Did he or she give everyone a chance to speak?

3 Did he or she keep to the agenda?

4 Did he or she give clear actions and were they summarized at the end of the meeting?

These are facts, and the behaviours are repeatable. They are useful for the person receiving the feedback.

Apart from giving feedback in terms of behaviour and effect, there are certain other points that should be observed. The equation should include a suggestion on how to do things differently. That is what makes feedback constructive, rather than just critical.

1 Do be descriptive.

2 Do be specific.

3 Take account of the needs of the receiver as well as your own.

4 Make the feedback well-timed.

5 Consider whether the feedback is about behaviour the person can change. Feedback on physical attributes such as accent is rarely helpful.

6 Check that the person has heard and understood the feedback. Feedback of either a positive or negative nature may be hard to accept, so people will sometimes distort the information you have given them, consciously or subconsciously.

Before giving feedback, always consider for whose benefit you are giving it, because it can be destructive if it serves only the needs of the person giving it.

1 If you think it is only to relieve tensions within yourself, do not give it.

2 If you do give feedback based on your perceptions, it is important to make it clear that that is what you are doing. For example, 'When you did "X", I wondered whether.../I got the impression you were feeling "Y".' Do not say 'When you did "X", you were feeling "Y".' The first example contains a safeguard in case your perception was wrong.

The skill in giving feedback is presenting the information in such a way that the person can accept without feeling embarrassed or humiliated.

Sometimes you might receive feedback yourself. It is not always easy to receive, as it can sometimes be hurtful. To obtain maximum benefit from any feedback you receive, the following steps can be helpful:

1 Listen carefully to what is being said.

2 Try not to let defences build up; mentally note any questions or disagreements.

3 Paraphrase what you think you heard to check that your perception is correct.

4 Ask questions for clarification in those areas that are unclear or with which you disagree, and paraphrase their answers.

5 Carefully evaluate the accuracy and potential of what you have heard.

6 Gather additional information from other sources, or by observing your own behaviour and people's reaction to it.

7 Do not overreact to feedback, but where you think change might be desirable, modify your behaviour, and assess the outcome of any modification.

8 Remember: feedback is just one person's point of view at one particular time.

9 You have the right not to act upon any feedback that is offered.

10 Don't get obsessive about feedback that is offered to you. Constantly eliciting feedback and acting on it can block spontaneity and creativity.

Questioning

Rudyard Kipling, in his *Just So Stories*, wrote this verse:

I keep six honest serving-men
(They taught me all I knew);
Their names were What and Why and When
And How and Where and Who.

Starting a question with one of these six words will elicit an answer that must be longer than 'yes' or 'no'. To obtain information or clarification, we need to use questioning skills.

1 The first important factor to keep in mind is not to use more words than are strictly necessary. Instead of 'I wonder if you could possibly explain to me' say 'Tell me how...' and instead of 'At what point in time did this happen?' use 'When?'

2 If the person is well known to you, then one or two questions on a subject he or she is interested in such as hobbies or holidays work well as good general 'ice-breakers'.

3 Openers such as 'How are the children getting on at...' or 'Did you all enjoy the holiday in...' will give the person you are speaking to the chance to settle into the environment.

4 If it is a person from outside the company or from a different office or branch, then a question or two on the journey or a mutual acquaintance will have the desired effect.

5 Do not ask questions or ask for opinions on contentious subjects such as politics or world events; this could wreck the whole session.

RELEVANCE

1 Make sure that the question refers to the subject matter.

2 When starting a questioning session, it is always a good idea to try to put the person being questioned at ease. One way is to ask some general questions on any subject.

3 Once it appears that the person is comfortable, stick to the subject matter.

4 If a group of people is asking questions, try to have a chairperson who can keep the session in order.

LANGUAGE

1 Try to use words so that the people you are addressing can understand the meaning.

2 If they feel that they do not understand, then they may be too embarrassed to ask you to repeat the question in a different way, or they may close down completely.

3 Make sure that your questions are concise and to the point. Too much extraneous 'waffle' may mean that the early part of the question is lost.

4 Try not to use words that are ambiguous or that could have different meanings for people in different situations.

LEADING

In certain circumstances, it may be necessary to lead the person being questioned along a route to obtain the answers that we think we need.

Leading questions can be dangerous but are sometimes necessary. To try to get the whole picture of an event(s), it may be possible to use opening questions such as, 'Could you tell me what you heard during the argument at the coffee machine' or 'What do you think was the basis for the disagreement in the car park?'

These questions show that you are aware that something happened but you would like more information upon which to base an opinion. Do not say, 'What was your part in...' or 'What did you say that caused....' Such phrases indicate that your mind is already made up.

1 They may be reticent or evasive due to misplaced loyalty or the fear that there may be recriminations if the full story is told. The only way to find the information is to ask leading questions. Examples include: 'Why did "X" take the action that he did?' or 'Were you aware that that "Y" spoke to...?'

2 Cautious use should be made of leading questions because it could be said that you 'put words into someone's mouth' or made a suggestion that the other person was unaware of.

3 Leading could also have the effect of closing down too soon a line of enquiry that could prove fruitful.

4 Some leading questions may be subtle. The questions are so worded that they may not appear to be leading questions, but they nevertheless lead to the response that the questioner desires. Market researchers often use this type of question.

6

dealing with questions

Open and closed questions

The three major types of question are known as open, closed and probing. Each one has a purpose, and we need to use them at the appropriate times in order to obtain as much information as we can. We will consider open and closed questions together because they are usually used in combination to achieve the responses required.

Open questions are those that require more than a 'yes' or 'no' answer, and help to draw more information from a person. They sometimes call for an opinion. A closed question usually receives a one-word answer, which sometimes is all that is required.

For several reasons, those being questioned do not always provide answers that fully satisfy the questioner. Is it the way that the question has been framed or asked? Is it because the person questioned has not fully understood the question? Or is it because the person questioned does not wish to communicate certain facts?

1 How the question is framed will certainly determine the response that is given.

2 In some circumstances, a question that warrants a 'yes' or 'no' answer will establish facts that should help to narrow down the enquiry.

3 This could be followed by another question of similar nature to further define the process.

4 We can thus establish whether there will be any benefit in proceeding with this line of enquiry.

5 In business, the main context for questions being asked and answers given is the interaction between manager and employee. It could concern the allocation of work on a day-to-day basis or to check on the progress of a particular task that was previously set. It could be in the more formal situation of the appraisal interview. In any of these scenarios, the principle is the same.

By way of example, consider the following situation in which an employee has been called to the manager's office.

Manager: 'Good morning X. Would you like some coffee?' (*closed question*)

Employee: 'Yes please.'

Manager: 'With milk and sugar?' (*closed question*)

Employee: 'No sugar, thank you.'

Manager: 'How would you feel about taking on the responsibility for...?' (*open question*)

Employee: 'How much more work would it involve?' (*open question*)

Manager: 'Quite a lot, could you cope?' (*answer followed by a closed question*)

Let us now analyze the exchange and see what effect the sequence has.

1   The manager's first two questions can be considered as ice-breakers. These are just 'pleasantries' to set the employee at ease.

2   The third question, 'How would you feel...?' should elicit a response that is more than just 'yes' or 'no'. It is asking for an opinion from the employee, without initially going into too much detail as to the content of the task.

3   If the employee gave an answer such as 'OK', then the manager would need to ask a further open question such as, 'What do you mean by "OK"?'

4   The final question in the series calls for a 'yes' or 'no' type answer to establish whether it is time to explain in more detail the nature of the task and attendant responsibilities.

There is no formula for the sequence of open and closed questions: it will depend on the situation and the type of responses that are given. Closed questions are easier to answer than open questions, mainly because they do not seek an opinion from the respondent.

As well as the 'yes/no' type of closed question, there is also the 'identification' type of question. This requires the respondent to identify a fact required by the questioner. An example of an identification question could be 'Where do you live?' which would require the respondent to state his or her address. Another could be 'What make of car do you drive?'

Closed questions have their uses, but they may hide the real reasons for the answer. Consider the following scenario: three managers are asked a question that has been posed by the board of directors. 'Should the company introduce a scheme for senior managers to have company cars?' Each manager answers 'yes', but that could have been for three different reasons.

1 The first manager answered 'yes' because there has been unrest about the lack of pay raises and this scheme could satisfy that wish. His figures have shown that the long-term effect of one could outweigh the one-time cost of the other.

2 The second manager answered 'yes' because she thinks that the external image of the company should be improved, and this would be a way of showing competitors that they were a growing company. There might also be a chance for some advertising if the company logo were displayed on a vehicle.

3 The third manager answered 'yes' even though he was opposed to the suggestion on the basis of cost. However, most of the company's competitors had introduced a similar system and this could be a way of preventing staff leaving to join a rival firm.

From these answers, the board could get the impression that all three managers favoured the scheme for the same reasons.

They might think that all three were committed to the idea whereas one was not in favour.

A survey is another example of the use of closed questions that can give hidden answers. It is usual to ask closed questions in a survey because without opinions the questions take less time to answer. For instance, a survey to establish the preference of pets for a certain brand of canned food might pose the following questions:

1 Do you have a pet?

2 Is it a cat or a dog?

3 Do you feed it on canned food?

4 Have you given your pet the brand X?

5 Did your pet like it?

All of these questions are of the 'yes/no' or 'identification' type.

Suppose for the sake of argument the outcome of the survey was that 12 did not respond, 15 did not have a pet, 13 of those who did have a pet did not have either a cat or a dog, 10 did not feed their pet on canned food, 15 of those with a cat or dog had not tried brand X and 20 said that their pet liked the product. How you use the answers will provide different results. Of the 35 cats or dogs that had tried brand X, 20 had liked it. This shows that 4 out of every 7 liked it, almost 60 per cent. However, of the 100 surveys, only 20 liked the product; therefore, on this basis, only 20 per cent showed a liking.

1 In an advertising campaign, which of the two results would it be wisest to choose?

2 How effective is the answer in helping someone who has not tried the brand?

dealing with questions

Closed questions can be regarded as manipulative as they do not seek an opinion from the respondent, but they can enable you to gather much more information from the individual who is answering.

Questions are often asked in a sequence. There are two sequences, called the funnel and the inverted funnel. The names derive from the shape of the questions.

1 FUNNEL
These go from open to closed questions.

2 INVERTED FUNNEL
These go from closed to open questions.

FUNNEL

Q: Why do you shop at Safeco's supermarket? (*open*)

A: Because it is closer to where I live.

Q: Why is that important to you? (*open*)

A: Because I can walk there.

Q: Is that because you do not have a car? (*closed*)

A: Yes.

INVERTED FUNNEL

Q: Do you shop at Safeco's supermarket? (*closed*)

A: Yes.

Q: Do you have a choice as to where you shop? (*closed*)

A: Yes.

Q: Why do you choose Safeco? (*open*)

A: Because I do not have a car and I can walk to Safeco's.

Probing questions

However careful we are in asking questions in the correct sequence or choosing the wording to elicit all the required information, there are going to be occasions when we need to delve further.

1 Sometimes it may be possible to prompt the respondent into a more detailed answer by simply accenting a pause, during which opening the hands, palms upwards, while maintaining eye contact will result in further explanation.

2 The use of verbal encouragement in the form of 'tell me more' or 'and…' or even just an 'uh-huh' will be enough without the need for further questioning.

3 We can also use the method of reflecting or paraphrasing that was explained earlier (see pp. 178–181). This will indicate our level of understanding of what has been said so far and gives the respondent the opportunity to amend, elaborate or clarify his or her previous answers.

Probing questions are used to encourage the respondent to be more forthcoming with answers. Probing questions must:

1 Allow the respondent, within the context of the question, to provide additional information.

2 Allow the existing relationship to be continued between interviewer and respondent.

3 Not fundamentally change the inherent meaning of the original question.

Probing questions take various forms and are used for specific purposes. They can be used:

1 To ascertain the accuracy of a statement, such as 'Are you sure that the words actually used were...?' or 'Did that follow immediately afterwards?'

2 To allow the respondent to add further information to the initial response, 'So what then happened?'

3 To better understand the answer given by asking, 'Why do you think it happened that way?' (*open question*) or 'Are you certain it was like that?' (*closed question*).

4 To illustrate the situation more clearly. 'Can you think of an example that will illustrate...?'

5 To ask the respondent to justify his or her answer. 'Why do you think that is the reason for...?'

Probing questions can be used in conjunction with open and closed questions and can be part of the funnel and inverted funnel sequences previously described. The skilled interviewer will know when and how to use these different types of questioning to obtain maximum benefit from the interview. As with most things, practise will help to perfect the technique.

Closure

When it is felt that the main purpose of the interview has been achieved, we need to ensure that there are no points that have not been examined and that both questioner and respondent have understood what was asked, said and discussed.

1 In order for the respondent to feel that he or she has contributed all that is possible, there needs to be some form of signal that the interview is about to close.

2 The questioner should feel that sufficient information has been obtained to satisfy the purpose of the interview and prepare to draw the session to a close.

3 Without a closure, the respondent does not know whether he or she is expected to answer more questions or leave the room.

ONE OF THE USUAL CLOSURES IS THE SUMMARY.

1 The summary benefits both parties.

2 It allows the interviewer to demonstrate that he or she has remembered the information correctly and confirm that the responder has been understood.

3 It also allows corrections to be made if the summary shows any errors and for additional information to be given if there are any glaring omissions.

Because summaries may have been used throughout the interview, it is important to signify that this is the final summary with some form of verbal indication: 'Just before we finish, let me summarize...' allows the respondent to take stock of the situation.

To be effective, the closure should also reward the respondent for his or her part in the process. The reward should be in the form of thanks for participation and an intimation that his or her input has been valuable. This will help to ensure that the respondent will be willing to take part in follow-up interviews if they are necessary.

In most cases, the interview will finish when all of the useful information has been gathered, but there are occasions when the interview must be ended because of other pressing matters.

1 Always be aware of how much time you have for the process and note the passage of time carefully.

2 Try to avoid the sudden 'I'm sorry, but we appear to have run out of time' end to the interview.

3   If time is a factor in the conclusion of the interview before all of the topics have been reviewed, try to arrange for a follow-up session on a mutually acceptable date. This can be helped by making the respondent feel that his or her contribution has been valuable, that something has been achieved and that a future session will be equally useful.

Other aspects of questioning

Other aspects to consider when questioning are sensitivity, culture and group questions. We will take these in turn.

SENSITIVITY

Try to be sensitive to the mood of the interview or meeting and especially to the other party(ies). Your not being aware of such feelings could result in answers that are not fully representative of the person.

1 How does the person appear? A person's appearance while being questioned sometimes gives a guide to current feelings. Anyone who is flushed or seems to be very warm may be feeling under pressure. Someone who is fidgeting may be feeling uncomfortable with the way the interview is going.

2 Is the person confident or hesitant?

3 Are you applying too much pressure?

4 Do you feel that there is something in the person's demeanour that is not usually there or that might be affecting the answers to the questioning?

5 Is your questioning overstepping the bounds of propriety? If you have overstepped the mark, apologize immediately. It is better to leave a brief pause before resuming questioning along different lines. If offence has been taken, bring the interview to a close, and reschedule for another day.

CULTURE
Always be aware of the culture of the participants.

1 In some cultures, asking questions in front of other people can be seen as a 'loss of face' or a sign of weakness. Frequently during a lecture speakers will invite questions from the audience but no one will ask one; however, at the end of the lecture a queue will form with audience members wanting to ask a question in private. This is also not uncommon in a business setting, where managers at all levels feel they might lose face, in particular in front of subordinates, by asking questions. Leaders should strive to ensure that they foster an open culture, in which asking questions is seen as making a positive contribution to understanding the 'big picture'.

2 In some countries, there seems to be a tendency to answer 'yes' to statements and questions. Beware, for this does not mean that a person agrees with everything that has been said or asked. The affirmation is only to show that the respondent has heard and understood the information. This can be a particular problem in parts of Southeast Asia and in Japan. If you are dealing with customers and suppliers in another country, always be sure to have an interpreter with you. It is easy to lose business through inadvertent misreading of signals.

GROUP QUESTIONS

Questions from a group need careful handling. It can be daunting to have to face a panel all with their own questions and sometimes their own agendas. Not knowing from which direction the next question will come and how it will be phrased can make any speaker's heart beat a little faster.

1 If possible try to ensure that there is one person who will take charge of the meeting and control how the questions are put.

2 Allow the respondent time to gather his or her thoughts if the questions are ad hoc.

3 If possible, try to give the respondent an idea of the subject matter prior to the session.

There are two situations regarding groups and questions:

1 The first is at a seminar or presentation where the speaker invites questions at the end of the session. The questions should relate to the content of the presentation, and the speaker should feel confident in dealing with them. If the answer is not known, the speaker should ask the questioner to leave a contact address and promise to find out and contact them. If the question is of a personal nature, the speaker should ask to speak to the questioner privately at the end of the question session. The speaker should never make fun of questioners or belittle them by referring to a personal attribute, such as size or dress.

2 Interviewing panels need to recognize the fact that the interviewee is at a disadvantage, and this will often show in the interviewee's demeanour. The chair of the panel should be sensitive to the type of question and the way it is put.

Used sensitively, questions and their answers can prove a most useful way of communicating and are very effective in eliciting facts, opinions and other information necessary in business.

Making a presentation

From time to time you may be asked to give a presentation, either to colleagues or to customers or suppliers. If you are not used to standing in front of an audience, this may seem daunting but here are some pointers to help you.

1 Always prepare your script well in advance. This will allow time for changes if more information is made available.

2 Try to become acquainted with the script so that you do not have to look down all the time.

3 Do some rehearsals on your own in front of a mirror at first until you feel more confident. Keep a note of the running time.

4 Prepare any visual material that you want to use to illustrate your talk. Do not use too many different media nor make your overlays for the overhead projector or PowerPoint slides too fussy. Remember to keep them simple.

5 Two or three days before the event, ask a few colleagues if they will sit and listen to you and comment on the performance. You may need to make some changes to the script.

6 On the day of the presentation, arrive at the venue in enough time so that you can set it up correctly or change the layout if necessary. Acquaint yourself with any equipment you intend to use, and make sure it functions properly.

7 If you have prepared handouts, wait until after the talk before you distribute them unless there is vital information in them that will aid your listeners' understanding.

8 Wear comfortable clothing, and relax. If you feel comfortable, you will be better able to make your presentation. Breathe normally and do not panic, even if something goes wrong.

Giving a press interview

If you are asked to talk to a journalist, weigh up the pros and cons before saying yes.

1 Be specific about whether your comments are personal or represent your organization's views. If the latter, give your job title.

2 Introduce the main points you want to get across immediately. This gives a reporter time to frame questions if he or she does not understand technical or scientific data. A short written handout may help to ensure that the facts or conclusions that are reported are accurate.

3 Don't criticize other companies or researchers: it's fine to say you disagree with someone's views or a report's conclusions, but don't dismiss individuals.

4 Use uncomplicated language. Reporters don't have time to research complex material: if the reporter understands, his or her readers probably will, too.

5 Avoid sensationalism: if you want your work reported in a serious manner, don't use words like 'conflict', 'stunning' and 'groundbreaking'.

6 If you can't answer a question, ask the reporter if you can call later, when you have gathered together the information you need. Be sure to ascertain the reporter's deadline, and stick to it.

7 You have the right not to answer any question, but it is probably more effective to deflect it.

8 Never make a statement you cannot support with facts and figures.

Talking to the media

Generally, the mass media do not want to know about your company. It is only when things go wrong that you become 'newsworthy'. An employee feels disgruntled and complains to the press. One of your products is faulty and causes damage. Company shares hit rock-bottom, and the future starts to look bleak.

If you have a public relations department they will handle these situations, but sometimes you will be the person who has to face the media.

1 Before talking to anyone, find out the facts. Are the alleged events true? What really happened?

2 What is the company policy on the matter? What actions have been taken so far?

3 Are there going to be any legal repercussions through what has happened? If so, what do the lawyers say?

4 If clear to do so, prepare a statement to hand to the media, and if faced by their representatives, stick to that statement.

5 If pressed do not offer any opinions; these could be misrepresented and used against you.

6 You do not have to say anything, but in the absence of facts, rumours will sometimes assume factual proportions.

7 Remember that a written statement, if misquoted, can be challenged, whereas opinions are subject to interpretation.

Summary

WHEN QUESTIONING

1 Use open and closed questions to obtain the information you require.

2 Use 'ice-breaker' questions to put interviewees at ease. This will produce better answers. Follow up on unexpected answers.

3 Probing questions will delve more deeply into the problem, but they may cause some upset when asked.

4 When you feel that enough questions have been asked, summarize the answers given to see if anything has been missed.

5 Be sensitive to an interviewee and 'read' body language, as well as listening to verbal answers.

WHEN YOU ARE QUESTIONED:

 Think carefully before answering and try to see if there is a 'hidden agenda'.

 Be aware that your body language could be sending different messages from your spoken answers.

 Try to keep cool no matter what is asked. The questioner might be trying to goad you into an uncharacteristic response.

If presenting to an audience, invite questions but do not worry if you are unable to answer any of them. You can always take a contact address or phone number and give the answer later.

Conclusion

1 Communication is the 'lifeblood' of business; we cannot exist without communicating internally and externally. Efficient communication will have an effect upon the 'bottom line' of our business.

2 The more efficient our internal procedures are, the less time we will take to perform all of the tasks necessary for a successful outcome. The less time we take, the less we spend. The 'buzzword' has to be 'right first time'. This applies to all internal communicating, both spoken and written.

3 A well-informed workforce usually perform their allotted tasks with the least amount of uncertainty, and this will be reflected in the products or services your company is providing.

4 Relationships with customers and suppliers depend upon the way we converse with them. Prompt responses to their enquiries by whatever means ensure that our company remains on good terms with them. This will result in repeat orders and shorter supply lead times.

5 A careless 'off-the-cuff' comment in an unguarded moment can undo all the good work on customer relations in a flash. Always consider the effect your words and actions may have on your listener. Let effective communication be your own and your company's aim.

Index